Worship Aids

Series I, Year 1

H. Burnham Kirkland

CSS Publishing Company, Inc., Lima, Ohio

For more information about CSS Publishing Company resources, visit our website at www.csspub.com or e-mail us at custserv@csspub.com or call (800) 241-4056.

ISBN 0-7880-1925-2   PRINTED IN U.S.A.

This volume is dedicated to the United Methodist congregations I have served. I am forever grateful for their positive responses to our worship services, for their willingness to experiment with new ways, and for their affirmation of the tried and true forms of our great heritage.

I learned a great deal from them, and I hope I was able to lead them closer to God through our worship services.

A sincere thank you to the congregations I served in:

> *East Norwich, New York*
> *Centerport, New York*
> *Darien, Connecticut*
> *Manila, Philippines*
> *Quezon City, Philippines*
> *Middletown, Connecticut*
> *Stratford, Connecticut*
> *Anchorage, Alaska*
> *Winter Haven, Florida*

Table Of Contents

Foreword

This volume contains Worship Aids for Sundays through the calendar year. Worship Aids based on a First Lesson text, a Second Lesson text, and a Gospel text are provided for each Sunday.

These Worship Aids are based on the Revised Common Lectionary — Cycle B. For each Sunday and for each of the three Lessons you will find a Call To Worship; a Morning Collect, which may be used either as a unison prayer or as a Prayer Of Invocation; a Prayer Of Confession; and two suggested hymns.

The hymns I have selected come mostly from *The United Methodist Hymnal* — 1989 edition. A few, where I have placed an asterisk, have been chosen from the 1966 edition of *The Methodist Hymnal*. Most of them are familiar and I am sure will be found in most denominational hymn books.

In preparing the Call To Worship for each service I have frequently used as a resource the Psalm designated for that Sunday by the Lectionary.

Those who gather for worship at an appointed hour generally arrive early and engage in a variety of activities such as meditation, fellowship, and prayer. When the time comes they need to be brought together to focus their attention on the act of corporate worship. This is best done, not by simply announcing the opening hymn, but by engaging the whole congregation with a Call To Worship.

The Morning Collect or Invocation unites the congregation as it invokes God's blessing on their worship.

Part of our corporate worship should also encourage those who have gathered to confess before God and one another their shortcomings, as they also seek the help of the Almighty in leading a better life. The Prayer Of Confession is designed with this in mind.

This volume is intended to assist the person preparing to lead the worship in these important parts of the service. May God bless your endeavors.

H.B.K.

First Sunday In December

First Lesson: Isaiah 64:1-9
Theme: Plea For God's Presence

Call To Worship

Leader: Let us come before the Lord our God who has revealed himself in ages past.

People: We come, remembering that God has done awesome deeds that we did not expect.

Leader: As we enter into God's presence we are reminded that the Lord is our Father.

People: Yes, we are all God's people, and we come to prepare ourselves for the coming of God's Son, our brother, Jesus Christ. Amen.

Collect

Almighty and Everlasting God, we come before you to prepare ourselves for the coming of the Christ Child. We know that it is not you who have hidden from us, but we who have failed to recognize your presence among us. As we welcome the Christ Child may we realize anew that you, O God, are indeed Immanuel — God with us. Amen.

Prayer Of Confession

O Lord, do not be exceedingly angry, and do not remember our sins forever. We all fade like a leaf, and our iniquities, like the wind, take us away from your holy presence. Forgive us, we pray, and create in us clean hearts. In Jesus' name. Amen.

Hymns

"Come, Thou Long Expected Jesus"
"Emmanuel, Emmanuel"

First Sunday In December

Second Lesson: 1 Corinthians 1:3-9
Theme: Thanks Be To God Who Strengthens Us

Call To Worship

Leader: Grace to you and peace from God our Father and the Lord Jesus Christ.

People: We give thanks to God who strengthens us with spiritual gifts as we wait for the coming of our Lord Jesus Christ.

Leader: He will also strengthen us to the end, so that we may be blameless on the day of our Lord Jesus Christ.

People: God is faithful; by him we are called into the fellowship of his Son, Jesus. Amen.

Collect

Almighty God, our Heavenly Father, we give thanks to you for those who journey with us to the Bethlehem manger. Together we wait expectantly for the revelation of your love for all humankind through your Son, Jesus Christ our Lord. Amen.

Prayer Of Confession

O God, we profess to be followers of our Lord, Jesus Christ, but confess that we are not blameless in our efforts to bear witness to his love in our speech and in our actions. Forgive us, we pray, and strengthen the testimony of Christ among us. Amen.

Hymns

"People, Look East"
"I Want To Walk As A Child Of The Light"

10

First Sunday In December

Gospel Lesson: Mark 13:24-37
Theme: Keep Alert — Watch

Call To Worship

As we prepare to celebrate Christmas we must remember that Christ often comes into our lives when we least expect him. As we worship this morning let us keep alert lest we shut the door of our hearts to his coming.

Collect

Heavenly Father, as we make preparations to celebrate the coming of our Lord Jesus may we not be found sleeping when there comes a knock on the door of our hearts and Christ seeks to enter. Surrounded by the secularization of this holy season, keep us alert to the true meaning of Christmas. Amen.

Prayer Of Confession

Holy Child of Bethlehem, we humbly confess that as we prepare for your coming our thoughts have been mainly on sending out holiday greetings and preparing our shopping lists. By the power of your Holy Spirit forgive our shortsightedness, and fix our attention on the earth-shaking and life-changing event we celebrate with your coming into the world. Amen.

Hymns

"Wake, Awake, For The Night Is Flying"
"O Come, O Come, Emmanuel"

Second Sunday In December

First Lesson: Isaiah 40:1-11
Theme: The Lord Comes With Power

Call To Worship

Leader: As we worship, prepare a way for the Lord to come into your life.

People: As we prepare, we will open a highway for our God to come.

Leader: Then the glory of the Lord shall be revealed, and people everywhere shall see it.

People: We know the Lord comes, and he will feed his flock like a shepherd.

Collect

O Lord God, we know that you have revealed yourself through your Son, Jesus Christ, as a God of power who rules by love, tenderness, and gentleness. Help us as we seek to understand your will for us, and prepare our hearts that we may truly welcome the coming of the Christ Child. Amen.

Prayer Of Confession

Almighty God, we confess that we have been more concerned with strengthening the power of our weapons of war than with feeding your children around the world who are starving. We seek to solve problems at home by increasing punishment rather than showing care and concern. Grant us the strength and the will to try your way as we prepare for the coming of the Prince of Peace into our world of turmoil. Amen.

Hymns

"Blessed Be The God Of Israel"
"Hail To The Lord's Anointed"

Second Sunday In December

Second Lesson: 2 Peter 3:8-15a
Theme: The Patience of The Lord

Call To Worship

Leader: While you are waiting for the coming of Christmas what are you doing?

People: We have come to worship our God that we might be better prepared for Christ's coming.

Leader: While you are waiting, strive to be at peace.

People: The peace of God which passes all understanding is what we seek.

Collect

Ever-present God, may this time of worship be an occasion for us to open our hearts to you. While we wait for Christmas as an opportunity to celebrate your coming into the world in human form, make us aware that you are always ready to show yourself to us. Amen.

Prayer Of Confession

Lord, we wait for a new heaven and a new earth where righteousness will reign, but we confess we have not been leading lives of holiness and godliness. We know that your Son came into the world to show us the way, but while we sing "Joy to the world, the Lord is come," we have failed to be faithful disciples. Forgive us, we pray, and through your Holy Spirit enable us to so live that we might help your kingdom to come, and your will to be done here on earth. Amen.

Hymns

"Savior Of The Nations, Come"
"Let All Mortal Flesh Keep Silence"

Second Sunday In December

Gospel Lesson: Mark 1:1-8
Theme: Preparation For Christ's Coming

Call To Worship

Leader: Christ is coming! Prepare the way of the Lord.
People: What must we do to make ready?
Leader: Repent and seek God's forgiveness.
People: We confess that we are not worthy to untie Christ's shoe-laces, but we come seeking God's mercy.

Collect

Lord, we are so accustomed to surfing the Internet and switching television channels that we find it difficult to concentrate. In this hour help us to fix our mind and heart on you that we might be ready for your coming. As we seek your forgiveness for past failures, show us the way to live fruitful lives that demonstrate our true repentance. Amen.

Prayer Of Confession

Lord, we are getting ready to celebrate that day when Love came to dwell among us. Even as we make our preparations to mark the power of love made known to us in Jesus Christ, we must confess that we have failed to love others as we love ourselves, and we have neglected to choose service to others over show and selfishness. Help us as we seek to be the people Christ freed us to be, we pray in Jesus' name. Amen.

Hymns

"All Earth Is Waiting"
"There's A Voice In The Wilderness Crying"*

Third Sunday In December

First Lesson: Isaiah 61:1-4, 8-11
Theme: The Good News Of Deliverance

Call To Worship

Leader: I waited patiently for the Lord.
People: He inclined to me and heard my cry.
Leader: He put a new song in my mouth, a song of praise to our God.
People: Happy are those who make the Lord their trust.

Collect

O Lord, our God, we come to worship you and give thanks for the promised coming of your Son to proclaim the Good News of salvation to all who will receive him. Give us receptive hearts, we pray, that we may be called oaks of righteousness and be used by you to build up the devastation of many generations. Amen.

Prayer Of Confession

Lord, we know that you love justice and hate wrongdoing, but we must confess that we have not always faithfully followed in the footsteps of our Master. Forgive our waywardness, and through your Holy Spirit may we be builders of your kingdom here on earth. Amen.

Hymns

"Send Your Word"
"Lift Up Your Heads, Ye Mighty Gates"

Third Sunday In December

Second Lesson: 1 Thessalonians 5:16-24
Theme: Prayer And Thanksgiving As We Wait The Lord's Coming

Call To Worship
Let us come before the Lord rejoicing as we anticipate the birth of Christ.
Let us come before our God with thanksgiving for he has blessed us beyond measure.
With praise and thanksgiving let us worship the Lord our God.

Collect
Praise be to you, O God, for you have delivered us in our time of need. You are awesome in your deeds among mortals. When we stumble and fall back into bad habits, your steadfast love, O Lord, holds us up. We come into your presence this morning with thanksgiving, Father, and we lift up our voices to you with songs of praise. Amen.

Prayer Of Confession
Loving Heavenly Father, our good intentions are to hold fast to what is good, and to abstain from every form of evil. But we are weak, Lord, and you know where the road leads that is paved with good intentions. Forgive us, Lord, and enable us to walk the path that is straight and narrow, but leads to your kingdom. Amen.

Hymns
"Lo, How A Rose E'er Blooming"
"Love Divine, All Loves Excelling"

Third Sunday In December

Gospel Lesson: John 1:6-8, 19-28
Theme: Called To Testify

Call To Worship

Leader: Sing to the Lord, bless his name.
People: We will tell of his salvation from day to day.
Leader: Declare his glory among the nations.
People: We will speak of his marvelous works among all the peoples.
All: We come to worship the Lord, our Maker, for he is our God!

Collect

We give thanks, O God, for the light that came to the world through your Son, Jesus Christ. As we prepare to celebrate the coming of that Light of the world, make us ready, we pray, to testify and bear witness to that Light which no darkness can put out. Amen.

Prayer Of Confession

O God, how can we bear witness to Jesus, the Light of the world, when we so often choose to live in darkness. Forgive our foolishness when we know the Light is there, but choose instead to grope in the darkness. Lead us once again with the Light, Heavenly Father, and then use us to testify to the saving power of that Light which came into the world when Jesus walked among us. Amen.

Hymns

"Go Tell It On The Mountain"
"Good Christian Friends, Rejoice"

Fourth Sunday In December

First Lesson: 2 Samuel 1:1-11, 16
Theme: God Promises David His Kingdom Shall Be Forever

Call To Worship

Leader: God's promises are sure.
People: We worship a God who is dependable.
Leader: The infant Jesus, whose birth we are preparing to celebrate, is the promised King who will reign eternally.
People: Praise be to God.

Collect

O God, we know that you will not take your steadfast love from us, and we give you thanks that your Son has come into the world to share our joys and sorrows. Through his life, death, and resurrection we know that he will reign eternally in the hearts of his followers, and of his kingdom there will be no end. Amen.

Prayer Of Confession

Lord, like David of old, we keep trying to build bigger and better churches where we can confine you as we go about the business of living as though you did not exist. Forgive us, Lord, and enlighten our understanding that we might open our hearts to you. Through your Holy Spirit enable us to be builders of your kingdom, we pray in Jesus' name. Amen.

Hymns

"Fairest Lord Jesus"
"Hark! The Herald Angels Sing"

Fourth Sunday In December

Second Lesson: Romans 16:25-27
Theme: Glory To God Through Jesus Christ

Call To Worship

Leader: Glory to God who is able to strengthen you.
People: Thanks be to God for coming among us through his Son, Jesus Christ.
Leader: Praise be to the only wise God made known to us in the birth of the baby Jesus.
People: We look forward with great anticipation to Christ's coming.

Collect

Gracious God, with gratitude we are prepared to celebrate your coming among us through your Son, Jesus Christ. As we focus our attention on the Babe in the manger, may we not forget the carpenter's son, the teacher on the hillside, the betrayal and crucifixion, and the resurrection, for it is through all of these we have truly come to believe in him as God with us! Amen.

Prayer Of Confession

Lord, we have been so preoccupied with traditional preparations for Christmas that we have almost forgotten the true meaning of this holiday. We come seeking your forgiveness and your help in reclaiming this time as a time of renewal. May our faith in you be strengthened, and may our lives be renewed as we fully realize your presence. Amen.

Hymns

"Angels We Have Heard On High"
"He Is Born"

Fourth Sunday In December

Gospel Lesson: Luke 1:26-38
Theme: The Annunciation

Call To Worship

As we come closer to Christmas, like many we ask ourselves, "How can this be?" As we worship may we hear the words of God's messenger reminding us, "Nothing will be impossible with God."

Come, let us worship the Lord, our God!

Collect

Lord, like Mary, we are often perplexed by your plans for us. As we come together we pray that like Mary we may come to the realization that we can put our trust in you. Like Mary, may we be prepared to hear your call and respond, "Here am I, the servant of the Lord, let it be with me according to your word." Amen.

Prayer Of Confession

O God, forgive us when we doubt your power. We confess that often we are tempted to handle life's problems our own way. Forgive our weakness, and may the power of your Holy Spirit enable us to respond to your call as we put our faith and trust in you. Amen.

Hymns

"To A Maid Engaged To Joseph"
"What Child Is This?"

Christmas Eve/Day

First Lesson: Isaiah 9:2-7
Theme: The Coming King

Call To Worship

Leader: The people who walked in darkness have seen a great light.
**People: Those who lived in a land of deep darkness — on them
light has shined.**
Leader: For a child has been born for us, a son given to us.
**People: He is named Wonderful Counselor, Mighty God, Ever-
lasting Father, Prince of Peace.**

Collect

Our hearts are bursting with praise and thanksgiving to you, Almighty God, as on this day we celebrate the birth of your Son, Jesus
Christ. He has brought light to our darkened world, and the hope of
the Peaceable Kingdom where love will reign supreme. Amen.

Prayer Of Confession

The babe whose birth we celebrate grew to be a man. Through his
teachings, the life he lived, and his death and resurrection, we have
learned that our God is a God of love and mercy. This light has shined
upon us, but we have often chosen to walk in darkness. Forgive our
foolishness, we pray, and enable us with the aid of your Holy Spirit to
show forth your love for all humankind. Amen.

Hymns

"O Come, All Ye Faithful"
"Angels From The Realms Of Glory"

Christmas Eve/Day

Second Lesson: Titus 2:11-14
Theme: The Purpose Of Christ's Coming

Call To Worship
Come, let us give thanks to our Heavenly Father, for the grace of God has appeared with the coming of his Son, Jesus Christ, bringing salvation to all.

Collect
Heavenly Father, we have waited for the blessed hope and the manifestation of the glory of our great God and Savior, Jesus Christ. Today we celebrate his coming as we mark the birthday of the Babe of Bethlehem. Thanks be to you, O God, for coming among us in your Son, Jesus Christ our Lord. Amen.

Prayer Of Confession
Lord, we know that your Son came into the world to teach us by word and deed to live lives that are self-controlled, upright, and godly. We confess, however, that though we earnestly try to be faithful followers of Jesus, we often fall far short of what we know to be the right way to act and do. We beg your forgiveness, Heavenly Father, and ask your help as we strive to walk in the light Jesus brought to us and all humanity. Amen.

Hymns
"Break Forth, O Beauteous Heavenly Light"
"Love Came Down At Christmas"

Christmas Eve/Day

Gospel Lesson: Luke 2:1-20
Theme: The Birth Of Jesus

Call To Worship

Leader: We gather today to celebrate with great joy the Good News.
People: Yes, for to us was born this day a Savior, who is Christ the Lord.
Leader: Glory to God in the highest,
People: and on earth peace, goodwill to all.

Collect

Almighty God, like the shepherds of old we have come once again to find the Christ Child. We open our hearts to him that he might abide with us always, and when our service has ended we will return to our daily tasks glorifying and praising you for all that we have heard and experienced this day. Amen.

Prayer Of Confession

O God, we are a cynical people. It is difficult for us to believe that a baby born in a stable over 2,000 years ago is the Savior of humankind. Forgive our disbelief, rekindle our faith, and through this beautiful time of celebrating the Nativity of Jesus, help us, like the shepherds of old, to go on our way singing praises to you for all that we have seen and heard. Amen.

Hymns

"Away In A Manger"
"There's A Song In The Air"

Fifth Sunday In December

First Lesson: Isaiah 61:10—62:3
Theme: The Good News Of Deliverance

Call To Worship
Leader: Our trust is in the name of the Lord.
People: We rejoice because of what the Lord has done.
Leader: Come, let us worship the One who has come to deliver us.
People: And sing praises to the God of our salvation.

Collect
Almighty God, we have welcomed the Christ Child into our hearts, and we will never be the same. We are new persons, and we are determined by the power of your Holy Spirit to be faithful disciples of our Lord. Amen.

Prayer Of Confession
Lord, we are your children, and part of your Holy Family. We confess that we have not always been obedient nor have we always done that which is pleasing in your sight. Forgive us, we pray, and help us to make amends. In Jesus' name we pray. Amen.

Hymns
"On This Day Earth Shall Ring"
"Sing We Now Of Christmas"

Fifth Sunday In December

Second Lesson: Galatians 4:4-7
Theme: God Sent His Son That We Might Become God's Children

Call To Worship

Leader: Praise the Lord all peoples.
People: Young women and young men, old people and children, too.
Leader: Let them all praise the name of the Lord!
People: His name is greater than all others. Praise the Lord!

Collect

Almighty God, through your Son, Jesus Christ, we have come to know you as our Heavenly Father. As your children you have blessed us beyond measure, and we come now to give you thanks and to praise your holy name. Amen.

Prayer Of Confession

Gracious God, we have sought to redeem ourselves by being good and law-abiding citizens, but we have failed. We now know that as your children we find our freedom from sin in your great mercy and forgiveness. Abide with us and strengthen us that we might serve you more faithfully. Amen.

Hymns

"Joy To The World"
"Christ Is The World's Light"

Fifth Sunday In December

Gospel Lesson: Luke 2:22-40
Theme: God's Child

Call To Worship

Leader: God has sent his Son into the world for our salvation.
People: Praise be to God.
Leader: We, too, are God's children, and have been sent to carry the Good News to all the world.
People: Thanks be to God. Amen.

Collect

As we come to worship you, O God, we give you thanks that like Simeon of old we have witnessed the salvation which you have prepared for all peoples. The Child whose birth we have celebrated is God's Child, and as your blessing was upon him we ask that it also be upon us. Amen.

Prayer Of Confession

Lord, when Simeon told Mary that many people would speak against your Son we wonder if he had people like us in mind. We have not spoken ill of you, but we confess that our actions have not always supported you or your message of love. Forgive us, we pray, where we have fallen short, and help us always to be true to you not only in word but also in deed. Amen.

Hymns

"Christ Whose Glory Fills The Skies"
"O Sing A Song Of Bethlehem"

First Sunday In January

First Lesson: Jeremiah 31:7-14
Theme: The Lord Gathers All His People

Call To Worship

Leader: Hear the word of the Lord, O nations,
People: declare it in the coastlands far away;
Leader: he who scattered the nations will gather them,
People: and will keep them as a shepherd a flock.
All: Praise be to God. Amen.

Collect

Father God, we your children have come together to offer our praises for your constant care. We give you thanks that as a shepherd cares for his sheep you lead us to still waters and green pastures. As we sing your praises and give you thanks may your Holy Spirit move among us to strengthen our faith and lead us in paths of service. Amen.

Prayer Of Confession

Almighty God, you have promised to guide and protect us if we will follow your will, but we have thought it was smart to be independent. We have insisted we know what is best, and have refused the leading of your Holy Spirit. Forgive us for our selfish ways that we may enjoy the freedom you have promised to all who follow you. Amen.

Hymns

"Hope Of The World"
"Jesus Shall Reign"

First Sunday In January

Second Lesson: Ephesians 1:3-14
Theme: Spiritual Blessings In Christ

Call To Worship

Leader: Come, let us praise God for his glorious grace.

People: We praise God for the free gift he gave us in his dear Son, Jesus Christ.

Leader: Come, let us give thanks to God the Father of our Lord Jesus Christ.

People: We thank God that through Jesus Christ he has made us his children.

Collect

Almighty God, Father of our Lord Jesus Christ, you have blessed us by giving us every spiritual blessing and chosen us to be your very own. As we come to worship you we seek a new awareness of your Holy Spirit that we may be used by you to further your plan to bring all creatures together with Christ as the head. Amen.

Prayer Of Confession

Compassionate Lord, we confess that we have fallen short of the expectations you have for us, and so we come humbly to claim the promise of forgiveness you have offered through your Son, Jesus Christ. How great is your grace, O God, which you gave to us in large measure. Amen.

Hymns

"Word Of God, Come Down On Earth"
"Jesus, The Very Thought Of Thee"

First Sunday In January

Gospel Lesson: John 1:1-18
Theme: The Word Of Life

Call To Worship

Leader: In the Beginning was the Word
People: and the Word was with God, and the Word was God.
Leader: God was in the world through his Son, Jesus.
People: But his own people did not accept him.
All: The Word became flesh and lived as one of us. Praise be to God!

Collect

O God, at Christmas time we celebrate the coming into the world the true light which enlightens everyone. Through your Holy Spirit enable us to walk in that light as your children, always seeking to do your will. Amen.

Prayer Of Confession

Lord, like those who walked with Jesus during his life here on earth yet did not know him as the true light of the world, we, too, have failed to recognize your presence among us. You have made yourself known to us through your Son, but we have failed to accept your will for our lives. Forgive us, we pray Father, and enable us to be bearers of your light in a dark world. Amen.

Hymns

"Wonderful Words Of Life"
"O How I Love Jesus"

29

Second Sunday In January

First Lesson: Genesis 1:1-5
Theme: The Beginning

Call To Worship
In the beginning God said, "Let there be light," and God said that the light was good.
With the birth of Christ a new light came into the world.
Come, let us worship the Light that no darkness can put out.

Collect
O, Creator God, we know that in the beginning you brought forth light to overcome the darkness, and in the birth of Jesus you brought forth the Light of the World that no darkness can overcome. We come now to give you thanks, for it is only through your Son, Jesus Christ, that we are able to find the way you would have us walk. In this hour may your Spirit touch each of us in ways that will enable us to go forth into the world with confidence and hope. Amen.

Prayer Of Confession
Almighty God our Father, we come before you with gratitude that our Lord Jesus identified with our sins through his baptism, and that he showed us your mercy and forgiveness. We come, therefore, with penitent hearts seeking your forgiveness for all the ways in which we have failed to be your faithful children. Amen.

Hymns
"God Created Heaven And Earth"
"Breathe On Me, Breath of God"

Second Sunday In January

Second Lesson: Acts 19:1-7
Theme: Baptism And The Holy Spirit

Call To Worship
John the Baptist came preaching a Baptism of Repentance in preparation for the coming of the Messiah.
Jesus came preaching a Baptism of Forgiveness and the Holy Spirit.
Come, let us repent of our sins, renew the vows of our baptism, and rekindle the Spirit within us.

Collect
Lord God, you have revealed yourself to us through your Son, Jesus Christ. We humble ourselves before you in this time of worship, and pray that as we think of the Baptism of our Lord, we may also reflect on the meaning of our own baptism. May your Holy Spirit come upon us once again, enabling us to live more fully and faithfully, as loyal disciples of our Master. Amen.

Prayer Of Confession
Dear God, so often it is the sins of the heart that do the most damage, and it is these very failings that we tend to excuse in ourselves. We remember this morning, with saddened hearts, the times when we have lost our tempers, said unkind things to those we love, and ignored the opportunities to be helpful to others. Forgive us, we pray, and by the power of your Holy Spirit strengthen us to show your love for all humanity by the way we act. Amen.

Hymns
"Come, Holy Ghost, Our Hearts Inspire"
"This Is The Spirit's Entry Now"

Second Sunday In January

Gospel Lesson: Mark 1:4-11
Theme: The Baptism Of Jesus

Call To Worship
At his baptism Jesus was recognized as the Son of God.
At our baptism we are recognized as children of God, brothers and sisters with Christ in God's family.
Come, let us worship the God and Father of us all.

Collect
O God, as we come to worship you we pray that we may be aware of your presence with us through the Holy Spirit. Open our ears to hear you speak to us through the songs we sing and the words we hear. Open, too, our hearts that, being warmed by your Spirit, we may be ready to go back to our daily tasks ready to witness to your love. Amen.

Prayer Of Confession
Dear Lord, we bow before you in contrition because we are unworthy of your great love; but we also come to you in gratitude because we have learned from you of God's great mercy and forgiveness. We come, therefore, with penitent hearts to claim that forgiveness through Jesus Christ, our Savior. Amen.

Hymns
"When Jesus Came To Jordan"
"Praise And Thanksgiving Be To God"

Third Sunday In January

First Lesson: 1 Samuel 3:1-10 (11-20)
Theme: Called By God

Call To Worship

Leader: Wait patiently for the Lord and he will hear your cry.

People: He will set my feet upon a rock, making my steps secure.

Leader: He will put a new song in your mouth, a song of praise to our God.

People: Happy are we who make the Lord our trust.

Collect

We come apart this morning, O Lord, that we might praise your name. We draw near to you and listen for your word for us. Speak to us, Lord, for we your servants are listening. Amen.

Prayer Of Confession

O God, how often you have tried to speak to us and we have not listened. Even worse, how many times we have heard your voice but refused to respond. Forgive us, Lord, and send your Holy Spirit upon us that we may not only listen when you call us, but also may respond with joy to your calling. Amen.

Hymns

"Here I Am, Lord"
"I Am Thine, O Lord"

Third Sunday In January

Second Lesson: 1 Corinthians 6:12-20
Theme: Glorifying God In Body And Spirit

Call To Worship
Paul wrote to the church at Corinth asking, "Do you not know that your body is a temple of the Holy Spirit within you?"

Remembering that God dwells within each of us through the Holy Spirit, let us present ourselves — bodies, minds, and spirits — before the Lord God Almighty whom we have come to worship.

Collect
O God, our Father, Creator and Sustainer of our lives, so often we come to you seeking renewal and strengthening of our spirits. This morning we come presenting our whole selves — body, mind, and spirit — asking that you will renew us, revitalize us, and awaken us to your presence within us, that we may better serve you in the days ahead. Amen.

Prayer Of Confession
We bow before you, Lord, in humble contrition, for we have treated our bodies as though they belonged solely to us. We have given in to our physical appetites, without considering the effect it would have on our well-being. We have failed to remember that we are stewards of our bodies, and that they are temples wherein dwells your Holy Spirit. Forgive our weakness, O Lord, and by the power of that same Holy Spirit enable us to be more faithful stewards of the body you have entrusted to each of us. Amen.

Hymns
"O Splendor Of God's Glory Bright"
"When Morning Gilds The Skies"

Third Sunday In January

Gospel Lesson: John 1:43-51
Theme: Jesus Calls His Disciples

Call To Worship
Like Nathaniel of old we come this morning with our doubts, our stereotypes, and our prejudices to hear what the Lord has to say to us.
Open your hearts and minds, and listen for what God has to say to you!

Collect
Heavenly Father, we call ourselves disciples of Jesus, but we come this morning with doubts and fears about our relationship to him and to you, O God. Speak to us in this time of worship, we pray, strengthening our faith and renewing our commitment. Amen.

Prayer Of Confession
O God, like Nathaniel, we ask, "How do you know me?" We have lived our lives as though we are completely independent. We have thought we had no one to answer to except ourselves. Now you have confronted us, and we realize that if we are to be faithful disciples we must strive to pattern our lives after Jesus. We seek your forgiveness, Lord, and the power of your Spirit to mend our ways. Amen.

Hymns
"Jesus Calls Us"
"I Surrender All"

Fourth Sunday In January

First Lesson: Jonah 3:1-5, 10
Theme: God's Call To Change Our Ways

Call To Worship

Leader: Wait in silence for God, for our hope is from him.

People: He alone is our rock and our salvation, our fortress; we shall not be shaken.

Leader: Trust in him at all times, O people, pour out your hearts before him.

People: God is a refuge for us. Amen.

Collect

Almighty God, we are gathered here to sing your praises and to give thanks for your creation. We also wait quietly to hear your word of judgment and your call to turn from our evil ways.

Speak to us now, Lord, and save us from ourselves. Amen.

Prayer Of Confession

O God, we pour out our hearts before you, humbly confessing that our actions and our behavior have fallen short of your will for us. Have mercy upon us, O Lord, and grant us the opportunity to try once again to be your faithful children. Amen.

Hymns

"Come, Ye Disconsolate"
"Give To The Winds Thy Fears"

Fourth Sunday In January

Second Lesson: 1 Corinthians 7:29-31
Theme: Time Is Short

Call To Worship

Leader: God is our shelter and strength, always ready to help in times of trouble.
People: So we will not be afraid, even if the earth is shaken.
Leader: The Lord Almighty is with us;
People: the God of Jacob is our refuge.
All: Praise be to God!

Collect

O God, we come this morning out of the confusion and uncertainty of daily life to sense the constant power of your love. We come realizing that for each of us life is short, and things are forever changing. In this time of worship, may there come a renewal of faith, hope, and love. May each one of us be equipped to go forth today determined to be part of the answer to life's problems rather than being part of the problem itself. In the power and guidance of your love this can happen for each of us. May it be so; in Jesus' name. Amen.

Prayer Of Confession

Father, by our poor commitment we have abused your mercy by continuing in our old ways. Lead us out of darkness into your marvelous light. Give us power to come alive in our witness to your wonderful deeds. We pray in Jesus' name. Amen.

Hymns

"Be Thou My Vision"
"Stand By Me"

Fourth Sunday In January

Gospel Lesson: Mark 1:14-20
Theme: Called To Discipleship

Call To Worship

Leader: Sing a new song to the Lord! Sing to the Lord, all the world!
People: Proclaim every day the Good News that he has saved us!
Leader: Proclaim his glory to the nations.
People: His mighty deeds to all peoples. Amen.

Collect

Lord, we have come this morning to worship you. We not only want to sing our songs of praise to you, and offer up our prayers of thanksgiving, but we would be still that we might hear your call to discipleship. By your Spirit grant us ears to hear and faith to respond. We pray in Jesus' name. Amen.

Prayer Of Confession

Lord, we bow before you with our record of mistakes and a sense of hopelessness. We know that we tend to do those things which we should not do, and leave undone those things which we should be doing. Wrap your arms around us, we pray, forgive us and set us free to be your disciples living in a positive way in your world. Amen.

Hymns

"Rise Up, O Men Of God"
"Christ For The World We Sing"

First Sunday In February

First Lesson: Deuteronomy 18:15-20
Theme: God Speaks To His People

Call To Worship

Leader: With all our hearts let us thank the Lord.
People: How wonderful are the things the Lord does!
Leader: All he does is faithful and just, full of honor and majesty.
People: His righteousness is eternal.
All: Praise the Lord!

Collect

O God, we come together this morning seeking to know your will for us. Speak to us through your Word and Spirit so that we may hear and respond to your call. We pray in Jesus' name. Amen.

Prayer Of Confession

Lord, we know that we are accountable for all that we do, and we confess that having heard your Word we often fail to show by our actions that we know your will for our lives. By your mercy forgive us, we pray, and enable us to live our lives in the spirit of your love. Amen.

Hymns

"Let My People Seek Their Freedom"
"Whom Shall I Send?"

First Sunday In February

Second Lesson: 1 Corinthians 8:1-13
Theme: The Responsibility Of Freedom

Call To Worship

Leader: The Lord has set his people free.
People: Holy and mighty is our God.
Leader: The way to become wise is to honor the Lord.
People: God gives sound judgment to all who obey his commands.

Collect

Lord, we give you thanks this morning for all those who have faithfully passed on your teachings across the years. Because we have learned from them we know that to truly love our neighbors we have a responsibility to so live our lives that we put no obstacles in the way of showing forth your love to all. May this time of worship renew our determination to bear a faithful witness to that love made known to us in Jesus Christ. Amen.

Prayer Of Confession

Lord, we have tried to show others how much knowledge we have about you and your will for all humankind, and it has made us feel puffed up and superior to others. We know better, for we have learned that we are called to show others how much you love them by the way we love them, too. Be merciful to us, we pray, and by your Spirit may we truly show forth your love by loving our neighbors as you would have us do. Amen.

Hymns

"Lord, I Want To Be A Christian"
"For The Healing Of The Nations"

First Sunday In February

Gospel Lesson: Mark 1:21-28
Theme: God's Holy Messenger

Call To Worship
Come, let us humble ourselves before the Lord God Almighty.
Come, let us behold God's Holy Messenger who teaches us as one who has authority.
Come, let us worship together.

Collect
O Lord, we know that you have made yourself known to us through your Son, Jesus Christ. Speak to us this morning through his teachings that we might learn your ways, and through your Holy Spirit give us power to so govern our lives that they may be pleasing in your sight. Amen.

Prayer Of Confession
Heavenly Father, the demons of hate, selfishness, pride, greed, and prejudice seem to take control of our lives. Come to us, we pray, through the power of your Holy Spirit, and cast out these demons by filling us with the love shown to us by your Son, Jesus Christ, in whose name we pray. Amen.

Hymns
"Jesus! The Name High Over All"
"At The Name Of Jesus"

Second Sunday In February

First Lesson: Isaiah 40:21-31
Theme: The Understanding God

Call To Worship

Leader: It is good to sing praise to our God.
People: It is pleasant and right to praise him.
Leader: He heals the brokenhearted.
People: His wisdom cannot be measured.
All: Praise the Lord!

Collect

Lord, we come to you in this time of worship weary and worn from our struggles during the week. We are weak and heavy-laden, and we feel powerless against the forces of evil that confront us. We wait upon you now, O God whose understanding is unsearchable, and ask that you will renew our strength, enabling us to mount up with wings like eagles, to run and not be weary, to walk and not faint as we go forth once again to confront the powers of darkness with the Light of the World shining in our hearts. Amen.

Prayer Of Confession

O God, often we are overwhelmed with self-pity. Confronted by trials and temptations we say you do not know what we are enduring, and that you have turned a deaf ear to our pleas for help. Forgive our lack of faith, we pray, and in this time together help us to regain our faith and confidence in your abiding presence. Through Jesus Christ our Lord. Amen.

Hymns

"Wellspring Of Wisdom"
"Be Still, My Soul"

Second Sunday In February

Second Lesson: 1 Corinthians 9:16-23
Theme: All Things To All People — Why?

Call To Worship

Leader: Great and mighty is our Lord.
People: His wisdom cannot be measured.
Leader: Sing hymns of praise to the Lord.
**People: He takes pleasure in those who honor him, in those who
trust in his constant love.**

Collect

God, you have entrusted each of us with the task of witnessing to
the Good News of your eternal love shown to us through your Son,
Jesus Christ. In this time of worship give us a new understanding of
what it means to be all things to all people so that some of them may
come to know you and your great love. Amen.

Prayer Of Confession

Almighty God, we are so self-satisfied, yet in our better moments
we realize how arrogant we must appear to you. We witnessed to your
great love, and from time to time, others are persuaded to accept your
love. When this happens we pat ourselves on the back and say we
have done a good job. Forgive our presumptions, Lord, and help us to
realize that it is not of our own power but only by your Spirit working
through us that we are able to be all things to all people for the sake of
the gospel. Amen.

Hymns

"O For A Thousand Tongues To Sing"
"I Love To Tell The Story"

43

Second Sunday In February

Gospel Lesson: Mark 1:29-39
Theme: Power Of The Good News

Call To Worship

When we let Jesus into our lives and into our homes we open ourselves to the healing power of God. In this time of worship draw near to God, and he will draw near to you.

Collect

Lord, help us in this time of worship to permit love to bring us newness of life. Just as the morning sun brings its warmth and fullness of life, so may your love come to bring a sense of refreshment and newness to each one of us. In Jesus' name we pray. Amen.

Prayer Of Confession

Heavenly Father, as we humbly seek your presence we come before you confessing our sins of commission and omission. Come with your healing presence, and according to your promise grant us your forgiveness. Through Jesus Christ our Lord. Amen.

Hymns

"Amazing Grace"
"Because He Lives"

Third Sunday In February

First Lesson: 2 Kings 5:1-14
Theme: Obedience to God — The Way To New Life

Call To Worship

Leader: Sing praise to the Lord, all his faithful people!
People: We will remember what the Holy One has done, and give him thanks!
Leader: The Lord will take away your sorrow and surround you with joy.
People: So, we will not be silent; we will sing praise to the Lord our God.

Collect

O God, we come seeking new life through your healing power. We come seeking strength and wisdom to obey your will. In this time of worship may we find both your healing power and the strength and wisdom to live as your obedient children. Amen.

Prayer Of Confession

God, our Father, we have let life become tarnished and less than beautiful because we have let our emotions govern us rather than letting your Spirit have full control. In this time of worship we ask that we may become more sensitive to your love for us, and that we may accept more fully your forgiveness and guidance. Amen.

Hymns

"Trust And Obey"
"'Tis So Sweet To Trust In Jesus"

Third Sunday In February

Second Lesson: 1 Corinthians 9:24-27
Theme: Run The Race To Win

Call To Worship
Let us come before the Lord our God that we might be better prepared for the race that is set before us. Seek the Lord while he may be found, and call upon him while he is near. Amen.

Collect
Almighty God, we come to give you thanks for your great love shown to us in Jesus Christ. We are determined to run the race of life in a way that will enable us to receive that imperishable prize promised to all who believe. We seek the power of your Spirit to so discipline ourselves that we might be better prepared to run that race. Amen.

Prayer Of Confession
Heavenly Father, forgive us when we have failed to have the discipline and commitment necessary to run the race of life with the intention of reaching the goal of eternal life. We have existed rather than lived. Now we seek your forgiveness, and the power of your Spirit to turn over a new leaf. We pray in Jesus' name. Amen.

Hymns
"I Sing A Song Of The Saints Of God"
"Victory In Jesus"

Third Sunday In February

Gospel Lesson: Mark 1:40-45
Theme: Jesus Restores Outcasts To Society

Call To Worship
Come to the Lord, all of you who are burdened and heavy laden.
With him you will find peace and newness of life.

Collect
We come to you, O God, with faith that you can help us if you
will. Have pity on us, we pray, and restore us to the fellowship of
those in our community that we may be renewed by your love given
to us through those who surround us. We pray in the name of Jesus
Christ our Lord and Savior. Amen.

Prayer Of Confession
We have been guilty, Lord, of losing hope. Our burdens seem
heavier day by day, and we have tried to carry them by ourselves.
How foolish of us. Now we reach out to you, God, and ask for your
help. May we turn our burdens over to you, Lord, and thus receive the
strength and power we need to face tomorrow. Amen.

Hymns
"Pass Me Not, O Gentle Savior"
"Come, Ye Sinners, Poor And Needy"

Fourth Sunday In February

First Lesson: Isaiah 43:18-25
Theme: God's Forgiveness

Call To Worship

Leader: The Lord says, "Do not cling to events of the past."
People: We will not dwell on what happened long ago.
Leader: The Lord says, "I am the God who forgives your sins."
People: We know the Lord will not hold our sins against us.
All: Thanks be to God for his forgiveness.

Collect

O God, we know that you do not burden us by demanding offerings or wear us out by asking for incense. We come this morning seeking your forgiveness and asking that you will make clear to us your will for our lives. Empower us, we pray, to be your faithful children. Amen.

Prayer Of Confession

We have sinned against you, Lord; be merciful to us and heal us. Help us to amend our ways that we may show by our actions that we are indeed your disciples. In Jesus' name we pray. Amen.

Hymns

"There's A Wideness In God's Mercy"
"Forgive Our Sins As We Forgive"

Fourth Sunday In February

Second Lesson: 2 Corinthians 1:18-22
Theme: God Says "Yes"

Call To Worship

Leader: Through his Son, Jesus Christ, God has promised that all who are weary and heavy-laden will receive rest when they come to him.

People: We come because God's promises are true.

Leader: Jesus also promised that those who seek will find, and those who knock will have the door opened for them.

People: We come seeking, confident that God will say "Yes" and open the door for us.

Collect

Heavenly Father, as your trusting children we know that we can count on your love. You have given us your Spirit in our hearts as a guarantee of all that you have in store for us. We come now to give you praise and thanks as we seek to know your will for each one of us gathered here today. Amen.

Prayer Of Confession

Lord, how often we have promised to be your faithful disciples, but our "yes" has also been a "no." Forgive our wavering commitment we pray, and enable us to show forth your love in all that we do. Amen.

Hymns

"O Jesus, Thou Art Standing"*
"I Sought The Lord"

Fourth Sunday In February

Gospel Lesson: Mark 2:1-12
Theme: Faith Heals

Call To Worship
It is not only our faith that makes healing possible, but also the faith of our friends. We gather then as a community of faith to support one another, and join our voices in praise and thanksgiving to the God and Father of us all.

Collect
We remember, O God, how in Jesus Christ you touched the lives of many who were suffering from brokenness of mind, body, and spirit. Your response of love to their faith and the faith of their friends brought wholeness and new life. We affirm our faith that Jesus is here with us to touch our lives and bring to each one of us a new sense of wholeness and power to live our lives in a positive manner. Help us, Lord, to be receptive to the healing and renewing touch of your love as it comes to us in Jesus Christ, our Living Lord. Amen.

Prayer Of Confession
O Lord, be gracious to us, heal us, for we have sinned against you. We know that when we seek your forgiveness you will be merciful and make us whole again. May we experience that forgiveness and renewal in this time of worship. We pray in Jesus' name. Amen.

Hymns
"Heal Me, Hands Of Jesus"
"Heal Us, Emmanuel, Hear Our Prayer"

First Sunday In March

First Lesson: 2 Kings 2:1-12
Theme: The Lord's Spirit Stays With Us

Call To Worship
May this time of worship be a mountaintop experience for you.
Let this hour transform your life as God reveals himself to you through his Son, Jesus Christ.
Come, let us sing our praise to God, and offer up our prayers of thanksgiving.

Collect
Our God and our Father, how wonderful it is that we can turn and call upon you. We know you as the very source of all that is, but more importantly we realize you are a gentle, caring, and loving Father who wants the best for each one of us. It is good to be able to come now, just as we are, and be assured of your accepting, forgiving, and restoring love. Amen.

Prayer Of Confession
Lord, when we are tempted to feel that you have deserted us and left us to our own devices, remind us that your Spirit is always with us. With the assurance of your abiding presence enable us to face life's difficulties with determination and hope. Amen.

Hymns
"Abide With Me"
"Sweet, Sweet Spirit"

First Sunday In March

Second Lesson: 2 Corinthians 4:3-6
Theme: Let Your Light Shine

Call To Worship

Leader: Jesus Christ is the Light of the World.
People: Let that Light shine through us.
Leader: We proclaim Jesus Christ as Lord.
People: It is for his sake that we are servants of our neighbors.
Leader: Come, let us worship our Lord and Master.

Collect

Almighty God, we come with open minds and hearts that we might better understand your Word. Speak to us that we may know your will as we go forth to let your Light shine through us that others may know the glory of God and his everlasting love. Amen.

Prayer Of Confession

Heavenly Father, sometimes we are so wrapped up in our efforts to live as loyal disciples that we forget it is not to show how good we are but to let your Light shine through us. We ask your forgiveness now, and pray that with your Spirit working in us we may keep our motives clear. Amen.

Hymns

"This Little Light Of Mine"
"Let There Be Light"

First Sunday In March

Gospel Lesson: Mark 9:2-9
Theme: The Transfiguration

Call To Worship

When Jesus was with three of his disciples on a high mountain they heard a voice from heaven say, "This is my own dear Son — listen to him." As we gather this morning for a mountaintop experience let us listen to what Jesus, the Son of God, has to say to us.

Collect

Lord, we have come apart this morning that we might get away from the distractions of everyday life and draw near to you. As we hear again the story of your Transfiguration may we realize that all those who have gone before us continue to live in you. Remind us again that we cannot dwell apart from the world in these high moments of spiritual insight. Empower us to go from this time of worship back into the world with the message that you are indeed the Son of God. Amen.

Prayer Of Confession

O God, in this time of worship we would confess our sins, accept your forgiveness, and renew our commitment. Touch us in your marvelous way, Lord. Then use us according to your will. In Jesus' name we pray. Amen.

Hymns

"Christ, Upon The Mountain Peak"
"O Wondrous Sight! O Vision Fair"

Second Sunday In March

First Lesson: Genesis 9:8-17
Theme: The Sign Of The Covenant

Call To Worship

Leader: Because the Lord is righteous and good, he teaches sinners the path they should follow.

People: He leads the humble in the right way, and teaches them his will.

Leader: The Lord is the friend of those who obey him;

People: and he affirms his covenant with them. Amen.

Collect

Creator God, you have shown us that you are a God of mercy and forgiveness. We know that your Son came into the world not to destroy, but to bring new life. We see the rainbow in the sky as a sign of your covenant to renew and reform us and your creation which we have often spoiled by greed and careless use. May this time of worship, Lord, be a time when your Spirit intercedes to remake and remold us according to your image. In Jesus's name we pray. Amen.

Prayer Of Confession

Merciful God, under the rainbow of your covenant we come seeking forgiveness for our sins and reformation of our lives that we might be a part of your creative process in the world rather than sharing in its destruction. Amen.

Hymns

"Seek The Lord"
"Great Is Thy Faithfulness"

Second Sunday In March

Second Lesson: 1 Peter 3:18-22
Theme: Christ Suffered To Bring Us To God

Call To Worship

Leader: Let us test and examine our ways, and return to the Lord!
People: God has blessed us; let all the ends of the earth fear him!
Leader: Seek the Lord while he may be found, call upon him while he is near;
People: let the wicked forsake their way, and the unrighteous their thoughts. Amen.

Collect

O God, who sent your Son into the world that everyone might be reconciled to you, grant that following the example of our Savior, Jesus Christ, and walking in the way which you choose for each of us, we may be united to each other and to you in holy love; through Jesus Christ we pray. Amen.

Prayer Of Confession

God and Father of us all, we were created by you to live in harmony with you, with one another, with the world around us, and with ourselves. By our own choices we have so often lived in discord, confusion, and weakness. Through your Son, Jesus Christ, you have come to us with outstretched arms of love, calling for us to live once again in harmonious relationships. We come now to receive your never-failing love and forgiveness. Amen.

Hymns

"My Hope Is Built"
"To God Be The Glory"

Second Sunday In March

Gospel Lesson: Mark 1:9-15
Theme: Temptation And Repentance

Call To Worship

Leader: Lift up your souls to the Lord.
People: We lift them up to our God in whom we trust.
Leader: Make us to know your ways, O Lord; teach us your paths.
People: Lead us in your truth, and teach us, for you are the God of our salvation.

Collect

O God, we have come together in the beauty of this place to renew our spirits and gain both guidance and strength for the living of our days. Like our Lord, long ago, we have faced our temptations. Help us now to put on that newness of life which you offer to us in Jesus, that we may live alive in the spirit of his love. Amen.

Prayer Of Confession

Heavenly Father, we have not always been as kind, patient, and loving with one another as you are with us. Forgive us, we pray, and enable us to witness to your love by the lives we live. In Jesus' name we pray. Amen.

Hymns

"O Love, How Deep"
"Help Us Accept Each Other"

Third Sunday In March

First Lesson: Genesis 17:1-7, 15-16
Theme: God's Covenant With Abraham

Call To Worship
Come, let us worship the God of Abraham and our God, too.
Let us give thanks to God who keeps his promises.
Let us praise the Father of our Lord Jesus Christ, and our Father, too.

Collect
Heavenly Father, we come into your presence this morning with praise and thanksgiving. We know that we have been blessed in many ways. Make us mindful that like Abraham we are blessed in order to be a blessing. Give us strength and courage to fulfill our responsibilities. Amen.

Prayer Of Confession
Almighty God, you have made us new persons in Christ, but how often we forget and live according to our old ways. Forgive us, we pray, and through the power of your Holy Spirit enable us to walk blameless before you; through Jesus Christ our Lord. Amen.

Hymns
"The God Of Abraham Praise"
"Great Is Thy Faithfulness"

Third Sunday In March

Second Lesson: Romans 4:13-25
Theme: The Example Of Abraham

Call To Worship
Come, let us give glory to God that like Abraham of old we might grow strong in our faith.

Collect
Eternal God, through faith Abraham believed that he would be the father of many nations according to your covenant. We come this morning as inheritors of that promise, and mindful that we are called to be a part of making it happen. Stir us by the power of your Holy Spirit that we may go forth from this time of worship determined to bring your Light and your Word to the nations of the world. Amen.

Prayer Of Confession
Heavenly Father, we thank you this morning for the gift of love, and most especially your love for us. Forgive us when we doubt the power of that love, and try to live by our own strength alone. Help us to dare to live victorious lives in the midst of defeat, joyful lives in the presence of sorrow, and in all things may our lives bear witness to the power and the presence of your love. Amen.

Hymns
"Guide Me, O Thou Great Jehovah"
"O Jesus, I Have Promised"

Third Sunday In March

Gospel Lesson: Mark 8:31-38
Theme: Cost Of Discipleship

Call To Worship
We have gathered together to worship God whose only Son gave his life for us.

We have come to turn our minds and thoughts away from human things that we might concentrate on divine things.

May God speak to each of us this morning according to our needs. Amen.

Collect
O Lord, may we hear your admonition to Peter when you said to him, "Satan, get away from me," as a warning to us not to resist your will because it does not agree with our view of worldly goals and ambitions. Strengthen our determination to seek first your kingdom. We pray in Jesus's name. Amen.

Prayer Of Confession
Lord, we confess that when we hear you talk about suffering and dying we tend to draw back and question the cost of discipleship. Forgive us, we pray, and give us a new understanding of what it means to be totally committed to you and your gospel. Amen.

Hymns
"Take Up Thy Cross"
"Where He Leads Me"

Fourth Sunday In March

First Lesson: Exodus 20:1-17
Theme: The Ten Commandments

Call To Worship

Leader: The law of the Lord is perfect; it gives new strength.

People: The commands of the Lord are trustworthy, giving wisdom to those who lack it.

Leader: The laws of the Lord are right, and those who obey them are happy.

People: The commands of the Lord are just, and give understanding to the mind.

All: May my words and my thoughts be acceptable to you, O Lord, my refuge and my redeemer!

Collect

Lord, once again we have come together to acknowledge you as our Heavenly Father, and to seek your blessing and guidance. Give us a new understanding of your commandments that we may walk as children of the Light, and be instrumental in bringing that Light to a dark world. In Jesus' name we pray. Amen.

Prayer Of Confession

O God, we like to think that we live upright lives, and that your commandments guide all our decisions. The truth is, however, that we fall short and constantly make excuses for ourselves. Forgive us, Lord, and strengthen our resolve to live according to your will. In Jesus' name. Amen.

Hymns

"God The Omnipotent"*
"Lead On, O King Eternal"

Fourth Sunday In March

Second Lesson: 1 Corinthians 1:18-25
Theme: Christ The Power And Wisdom Of God

Call To Worship
Come let us worship together, for here we proclaim Christ the power of God and the wisdom of God.

Collect
Almighty and Everlasting God, often we have looked for miracles to show us your power, and we have turned to those the world calls wise to discover your wisdom. This morning we gather to worship you through Jesus Christ our Lord who has shown us your true power and wisdom. Praise be to you, O God. Amen.

Prayer Of Confession
We know, Lord, that you accept us as we are despite our foolish ways. We know, too, that we more readily follow the ways of the world than we follow your ways. Forgive our shortcomings, Lord, and help us so that we may learn to value your wisdom over the wisdom of the world. Amen.

Hymns
"The Old Rugged Cross"
"Lift High The Cross"

Fourth Sunday In March

Gospel Lesson: John 2:13-22
Theme: Let Your Devotion To God Burn In Your Life Like A Fire

Call To Worship
Leader: Come, let us worship the Christ.
People: With his coming we are healed. Through him we are one in the Spirit.
Leader: Come, let us worship, offering him voices and lives in harmony with his will.
People: We will give of ourselves in service to God and to his people. Amen.

Collect
We are thankful, Lord, that you are present with us. When we are weary you strengthen us. When we are upset you bring calm to our troubled souls; our fears subside, and our hearts are filled with peace. Give us courage, Lord, that when we confront evil we may resist it, counting not the cost of our decision, but only the inward joy that awaits those who choose to follow you. Amen.

Prayer Of Confession
O Christ of the cross, we bow in contrition before you confessing our failures. We have commercialized your church and compromised our faith. We have concentrated on budgets and fund-raising, rather than serving you by ministering to the needs of your children. Forgive our self-righteousness that ignores the need for sacrifice and servanthood, and cleanse us by the power of your Holy Spirit. Amen.

Hymns
"Grace Greater Than Our Sin"
"There's Within My Heart A Melody"

Fifth Sunday In March

First Lesson: Numbers 21:4-9
Theme: When We Lose Patience

Call To Worship
When life seems to close in upon us, and we lose patience with God for not answering our prayers, remember that God's faithfulness endures and the power of his Spirit will see us through.
Come, let us worship our dependable God.

Collect
Almighty God, open our ears and our hearts to hear the cries of the needy. Strengthen our resolve to remember them in prayer, and guide our actions that we may be your agents of grace and mercy bringing to them salvation of both body and soul. Amen.

Prayer Of Confession
Lord, we confess that we are not only an impatient people, but we are quick to complain. We bemoan our lot in life when we should be counting our blessings. When we do not have all the material things we think are our due, we fail to see all the intangible blessings that are ours — like freedom, companionship, and love. Forgive our short-sightedness and give us grateful hearts. We pray in Jesus' name. Amen.

Hymns
"In The Cross Of Christ I Glory"
"Thou Hidden Source Of Calm Repose"

Fifth Sunday In March

Second Lesson: Ephesians 2:1-10
Theme: New Life In Christ

Call To Worship

Leader: Give thanks to the Lord, because he is good;

People: his love is eternal.

Leader: We were living in gloom and darkness, because we had rebelled against the commands of Almighty God.

People: We must thank the Lord for his constant love, for the wonderful things he did for us.

Leader: We were fools, suffering because of our sins and because of our evil.

People: We must thank the Lord for his constant love, for the wonderful things he did for us. Amen.

Collect

Heavenly Father, thank you for never giving up on us, even when we are intent on giving up on you. When in our despair we have turned to you, you have given us another chance, a new life of joy and service, of sharing and love. We come therefore to give you thanks and to praise your Holy Name. Amen.

Prayer Of Confession

O God, once we were like everyone else, following the desires of flesh and senses. Then, Lord, your Son, Jesus Christ, came into our lives showing us the great love you have for us, and the richness of your mercy. Humbly we offer our prayer of thanksgiving that you have turned our lives around, and pray that by the power of your Spirit we may be able to show your love to others. Amen.

Hymns

"Let Us Plead For Faith Alone"
"I Know Whom I Have Believed"

Fifth Sunday In March

Gospel Lesson: John 3:14-21
Theme: God's Great Love For Us

Call To Worship

Leader: Everyone who believes in Christ will have eternal life.
People: For God so loved the world that he gave his only Son, so that everyone who believes in him may not die but have eternal life.
Leader: The Light has come into the world, but people love the darkness rather than the Light.
People: Those who do what is true come to the Light in order that the Light may show that what they did was in obedience to God. Amen.

Collect

Gracious God, we know that we cannot earn your love or forgiveness, nor do we deserve it. However, we come with gratitude and thanksgiving to praise you for the gift of your Son, who through his death and resurrection has given us new life and the promise of eternal life with you. Amen.

Prayer Of Confession

Gracious Lord, we are truly grateful for the gift of new life you hold out to us. We are proud to be a part of your kingdom, but we confess that we have been slow to accept the responsibilities that come with your gifts. We rejoice that we can dwell in the light of your forgiveness, but we are slow to share your love with those who are lost in loneliness and despair. We have failed to bring the light of Christ into their joyless lives. Renew a right spirit within us, O God, and send us forth determined, as children of the Light, to shed that Light abroad. In Jesus's name we pray. Amen.

Hymns

"O How I Love Jesus"
"My God, I Love Thee"

First Sunday In April

First Lesson: Jeremiah 31:31-34
Theme: A New Covenant

Call To Worship
Leader: Create pure hearts in us, O God,
People: and put new and loyal spirits in us.
Leader: Do not banish us from your presence;
People: do not take your Holy Spirit away from us.
Leader: Give us again the joy that comes from your salvation,
People: and make us willing to obey you. Amen.

Collect
Compassionate Lord, we bow before you in adoration and thanksgiving. We know that in keeping with your promise you have forgiven us our sins and no longer remember our wrongs. We rejoice in the new covenant you have made with us in Jesus Christ, your Son and our Redeemer. Bless this time of worship, we pray, and through it renew a right spirit within us. Amen.

Prayer Of Confession
Eternal God and Father of all humankind, we look forward to that day when all your people know you and obey your laws. We confess, Lord, that we are partly to blame that day has not yet come for we have failed to share the Good News of your forgiving love with our neighbors. Be patient with us, O God, and by the power of your Spirit make us instruments in hastening the day when every knee shall bow and every tongue confess that Jesus Christ is Lord. Amen.

Hymns
"From All That Dwell Below The Skies"
"O Zion Haste"

First Sunday In April

Second Lesson: Hebrews 5:5-10
Theme: Reverent Submission

Call To Worship
Life can be difficult. There is pressure on every side to conform to what the world around you wants rather than to what God wants. Jesus felt every pressure you feel. He knew disappointment and heartbreak. That is why you can bring everything to him. He knows what you are going through, and he cares.
Let us come before the Lord!

Collect
Lord of the universe, you have taught us how to live in harmony with you and with one another. You have not only given us direction, but you have also come to us in Jesus Christ to walk with us through the valleys and the storms of life. We gather this day to praise you for all your goodness, and to seek for a renewal of our own faith. Amen.

Prayer Of Confession
O God, we are so self-satisfied and afraid of losing our self-esteem that we have failed to humble ourselves before you. When suffering has come upon us we have complained to you rather than learning to be obedient sons and daughters, relying on your power and mercy to see us through our difficulties. Forgive us, Lord, and help us to bow in reverent submission to your will. Amen.

Hymns
"If Thou But Suffer God To Guide Thee"
"All Praise To Thee, For Thou, O King Divine"

First Sunday In April

Gospel Lesson: John 12:20-33
Theme: Lost And Found

Call To Worship
Seek the Lord while he may be found, call upon him while he is near; let the wicked leave their way of life and change their way of thinking. Let them turn to the Lord, our God, for he is merciful and quick to forgive. Amen.

Collect
Almighty God, we are so intent on saving our time, our strength, our talents lest we lose or waste them. This morning help us to see that we cannot find life's real meaning unless we are willing to lose ourselves in service to Christ and his kingdom. Amen.

Prayer Of Confession
O Creator God, you have given us life. You have blessed us immeasurably with gifts that enable us to make this world a better place for our children and grandchildren. Temptations to use these gifts for our own benefit often lead us astray. Strengthen and guide us, we pray, that we may know we have a divine purpose in life to lose ourselves in your service by sharing your love and your will for all humanity. Amen.

Hymns
"Amazing Grace"
"He Touched Me"

Palm/Passion Sunday

First Lesson: Isaiah 50:4-9a
Theme: Trusting The Lord

Call To Worship

Leader: Sing praise to God who has shown his love for us through his Son, Jesus Christ.

People: His love is a shelter in the storm and a light in the darkness.

Leader: If we will listen, his presence will direct our lives.

People: We will indeed listen to him, and we will go where he leads us.

Leader: Come, let us worship together!

Collect

Lord, we come to you with grateful hearts for the way in which you have sustained and strengthened us in all the trials and tribulations we confront. We ask now that you will give us the tongue of a teacher that from our experience and our growing faith in you we can strengthen the weary. In Jesus' name we pray. Amen.

Prayer Of Confession

God of all the ages, we need the forgiveness you have promised to those who turn to you. We know how Christ suffered for us, and how many of his disciples willingly bore the pains of persecution. But as for us, we prefer to avoid suffering and would rather choose the way of ease. Forgive us, we pray, and open our hearts and minds to the lessons to be learned from the things that cause us to suffer. Amen.

Hymns

"Only Trust Him"
"He Leadeth Me"

Palm/Passion Sunday

Second Lesson: Philippians 2:5-11
Theme: Imitating Christ's Humility

Call To Worship
When Jesus made his triumphal entry into Jerusalem he did not ride a big white stallion as military conquerors were accustomed to doing. Rather, he humbled himself and rode a colt, the foal of a donkey. Jesus was humble and walked the path of obedience all the way to his death — his death on a cross.

Come, let us sing our hosannas to Christ our Savior.

Collect
We thank you, Father God, that your Son became like a human being and appeared in human likeness. Because of this, O God, we know that you understand us and are well aware of the difficulties we face as we strive to do your will and share your love and concern with others.

We praise your holy name, O God, and give thanks for Jesus Christ, our Lord and Savior. Amen.

Prayer Of Confession
O God, we make endless excuses for our weakness, and when we give in to temptation we say it is only human. Yet we know that your Son, Jesus Christ, was human even as we are, but he did not yield to temptation. Forgive our weakness, we pray, and by your Spirit enable us to follow more closely the way Jesus has shown us. Amen.

Hymns
"All Glory, Laud, And Honor"
"What Wondrous Love Is This"

Palm/Passion Sunday

Gospel Lesson: Mark 14:1—15:47 or Mark 15:1-39 (40-47)
Theme: Jesus Is Crucified

Call To Worship

Leader: And the disciples began to rejoice and praise God, saying:
People: Hosanna to the son of David!
Leader: Blessed is the King who comes in the name of the Lord!
People: Blessed be the kingdom of our father David that is coming!
Leader: Hosanna!
People: Hosanna in the highest!

Collect

Lord, we are reminded today how shallow are our loud hosannas unless we support them with the costly sacrificial gifts of our lives. Let the Lord of life enter our lives this day, and may we in joyful homage lay ourselves before him as servants of the King. Amen.

Prayer Of Confession

Lord, we are too prone to follow the crowd. We let others decide for us when it is appropriate to take a stand. Forgive our weakness, we pray, and strengthen our determination to do those things that further the coming of your kingdom regardless of the cost to our own comfort. In Jesus' name we pray. Amen.

Hymns

"Hosanna, Loud Hosannas"
"O Sacred Head, Now Wounded"

Thursday In Holy Week

First Lesson: Exodus 12:1-4 (5-10), 11-14
Theme: A Day Of Remembrance

Call To Worship

Leader: The first Passover was to be celebrated as a Day of Remembrance that God spared his people by the blood of the sacrificial lamb.

People: We remember. Praise be to God!

Leader: The Last Supper was to be celebrated as a Day of Remembrance that God spared not his Son in order that his children might know his love and learn to serve him.

People: We remember. Praise be to God!

Leader: You who call upon the name of Christ, we are gathered to recall the story of the night Jesus Christ was betrayed. Are you prepared to come to the table of Jesus Christ whose life was poured out for you?

People: By the grace of God, we are!

Collect

Almighty God, you led your people out of bondage in Egypt so long ago. Now we come to you seeking freedom from sin that we might more worthily serve you by serving others. Bless this time of Remembrance, we pray, and as we come to your Table may it be for us a means of grace. Amen.

Prayer Of Confession

You have given us new life, O Lord. For such a great gift we should be ever thankful. Yet, we quickly take it for granted. We see our lives in terms of special privileges, and forget our responsibilities. Forgive us, Lord, for neglecting to use our gifts for your glory, for thinking only of ourselves. Help us to turn our privileges into action, not thinking about the risks involved but only desiring to serve you and work for your glory. Amen.

Hymns

"The Bread Of Life For All is Broken"
"O Crucified Redeemer"

Thursday In Holy Week

Second Lesson: 1 Corinthians 11:23-26
Theme: The Institution Of The Lord's Supper

Call To Worship
Christ calls us to join him at this Table of Remembrance.
The Lord asks us to watch with him in his passion.
Jesus showed us by example that we are to serve each other.
Come, let us accept the Master's invitation, and let us Remember!

Collect
In coming to your Table, O Lord, we sense our union with the community of believers spanning all time and all places. We remember, with humility, your passion and crucifixion. As we partake of the Bread and the Cup speak to us again of your great sacrifice for us, and renew in us the spirit of servanthood that we might show forth your love to others. Amen.

Prayer Of Confession
Most Merciful God, we confess that we live such busy lives that there seems to be little time for Remembrance of your great love shown to us through your Son, Jesus Christ. Forgive our preoccupation with trivial things, and by your Spirit make us faithful in every time of trial; through Jesus Christ our Lord. Amen.

Hymns
"For The Bread Which You Have Broken"
"Jesus, Keep Me Near The Cross"

Thursday In Holy Week

Gospel Lesson: John 13:1-17, 31b-35
Theme: A New Commandment

Call To Worship
Christ our Lord invites to his Table all who love him, who earnestly repent of their sin and seek to live in peace with one another. Christ has prepared a feast of love. Come, let us join him.

Collect
O God, who by the example of your Son, our Savior Jesus Christ, has taught us the greatness of true humility, and does call us to watch with him in his passion: give us grace to serve one another in all lowliness, and to enter into the fellowship of his suffering. Once again remind us of your commandment to love one another as you love us, so that everyone will know that we are indeed your disciples. Amen.

Prayer Of Confession
Most Merciful God, we confess that we have failed to love one another as Christ loves us. We have pledged loyalty to him with our lips, and then betrayed, deserted, or denied him. Forgive us, we pray, and by your Spirit keep us faithful to you in all that we do. Amen.

Hymns
"Jesu, Jesu"
"Because Thou Hast Said"

Good Friday

First Lesson: Isaiah 52:13—53:12
Theme: The Suffering Servant

Call To Worship

Leader: He was despised and rejected by others.
People: A man of suffering and acquainted with grief.
Leader: He was wounded for our transgressions, crushed for our iniquities.
People: The Lord has laid on him the iniquity of us all.
All: Behold the Lamb of God, which taketh away the sin of all the world. Amen.

Collect

Almighty God, your Son Jesus Christ was lifted high upon the cross so that he might draw the whole world to himself. Grant that we, who glory in his death for our salvation, may also glory in his call to take up our cross and follow him; through Jesus Christ our Lord. Amen.

Prayer Of Confession

O God, in this hour of solemn remembrance we acknowledge with sorrow and shame that our sins are such as sent our blessed Lord to the cross. We know that you are gracious and merciful, slow to anger, and abounding in steadfast love, and so we beseech your forgiveness. Lord, have mercy upon us. Amen.

Hymns

"When I Survey The Wondrous Cross"
"'Tis Finished! The Messiah Dies"

Good Friday

Second Lesson: Hebrews 10:16-25
Theme: Trust God To Keep His Promise

Call To Worship
Let us draw near to God with a sincere heart and a sure faith.
Let us hold firmly to the hope we profess, because we trust God to keep his promise. Amen.

Collect
Heavenly Father, on the cross Jesus showed us how to forgive. While he walked among us he taught us that we must forgive even as we are forgiven. Even as we have faith in your promise of forgiveness, we stand beneath the cross of Jesus and ask your help as we seek to follow the example of Jesus in forgiving our enemies.

Prayer Of Confession
We read in the Bible that we should be concerned for one another, help one another, show love, do good, and encourage each other. When we look back on how we have acted among our family, friends, neighbors, and strangers we realize how much we have fallen short of the mark. Forgive us, we pray, and grant us new opportunities to make amends. In Jesus' name we pray. Amen.

Hymns
"O Love Divine, What Hast Thou Done"
"Beneath The Cross Of Jesus"

Good Friday

Gospel Lesson: John 18:1—19:42
Theme: The Trial And Crucifixion

Call To Worship
On this day of gloom and despair when we mark the arrest, the trial, and the crucifixion of Jesus we call it *Good* Friday because we know the end of the story.
May our sorrow be turned to joy as we follow the Way of the Cross.

Collect
O God, our Father, as we go through life we suffer many injustices. In our despair we cry out, "Life is not fair." We thank you, God, for your Son Jesus Christ who came among us, endured the pain and suffering of an unjust society, but never lost his faith, hope, and trust in you. May we learn from his example! Amen.

Prayer Of Confession
O God, we pray your forgiveness for our blind and selfish ways. We fail to perceive the connection between our actions, or failures to act, and gross injustices perpetrated by our society because we do not want to acknowledge our guilt. Open our eyes, Lord, that we may see, our hearts that we may love, and our minds that we may have the wisdom to live as Jesus taught us. Amen.

Hymns
"Alas! And Did My Savior Bleed"
"Were You There?"

Easter Sunday

First Lesson: Acts 10:34-43
Theme: God Has No Favorites

Call To Worship

Leader: God raised Jesus on the third day, and allowed him to appear to those who would be witnesses.
Come, let us celebrate the Risen Lord, and prepare ourselves to witness to his amazing love.

People: Christ is risen! Hallelujah!

Collect

We give thanks for Peter's insight, O God, that you treat everyone on the same basis. We rejoice in the revelation that anyone who faces you and does what is right is acceptable to you regardless of race or nationality. We praise you, Lord, for the promise of eternal life made known to us through the Risen Christ. May we be faithful witnesses to this gospel, we pray in Jesus' name. Amen.

Prayer Of Confession

Lord, like some of your first disciples, we, too, often have questions and doubts about the resurrection. Come to us in our everyday activities that we, too, may experience for ourselves your living presence. Strengthen our faith that you are available to everyone, and make us to be faithful witnesses to your great love. In Jesus' name. Amen.

Hymns

"Christ Is Risen"
"Hail The Day That Sees Him Rise"

Easter Sunday

Second Lesson: 1 Corinthians 15:1-11
Theme: Resurrection

Call To Worship

Leader: This is Easter — Hallelujah!
People: Christ rose from the dead. Praise be to God!
Leader: His resurrection is the proof of our resurrection — Hallelujah!
People: Christ is alive and we will live with him forever. Praise be to God!

Collect

Lord, we do not fully understand the Easter event, but we do know that through it we have come to know you as a living, loving God who walks with us and talks with us, and tells us that we are your own. In loving gratitude for such love we offer ourselves as a living sacrifice to your kingdom so that others may come to experience the Easter event in their lives. Amen.

Prayer Of Confession

Eternal God who has shown us glimpses of eternity through the resurrection of your Son, Jesus Christ, we confess that death still mystifies us. There is something fearsome about death and grievous in the separation it brings between the living and the dead. We want to overcome our doubts about resurrection. Help us to receive the witness of your apostles that even we may experience the presence of the Living Christ in whose name we pray. Amen.

Hymns

"Thine Be The Glory"
"The Day Of Resurrection"

Easter Sunday

Gospel Lesson: John 20:1-18 or Mark 16:1-8
Theme: The Resurrection

Call To Worship

Leader: Christ is risen!
People: Christ is risen indeed! Alleluiah!
Leader: Jesus said, "I am the resurrection and the life.
People: Those who believe in me, even though they die, will live, and everyone who lives and believes in me will never die."
All: Praise be to God!

Collect

Almighty God, who through your only Son overcame death, and opened to us the gate of everlasting life: grant that we who celebrate our Lord's resurrection may by the renewing of your Spirit arise from the death of sin to the life of righteousness; through the same Jesus Christ our Lord. Amen.

Prayer Of Confession

Lord, so often we come to you in prayer and then turn away because we do not recognize your voice speaking to us. Open our hearts to your presence, we pray, and through your Spirit help us to hear you speak your words of hope, comfort, and challenge. Amen.

Hymns

"Christ The Lord Is Risen Today"
"He Lives"

Fourth Sunday In April

First Lesson: Acts 4:32-35
Theme: The Blessedness Of Unity

Call To Worship

Leader: How wonderful it is, how pleasant for God's people to live together in harmony!

People: The Lord has promised his blessing — life that never ends.

All: Thanks be to God!

Collect

Lord, we know that before your death you commanded your followers to love one another. Following your resurrection the believers lived together in harmony, and no one in the group was in need. We come this morning rejoicing in your living presence among us, and asking that your Spirit may stir up within us that love for each other which will bring about the blessedness of unity which is pleasing to you. Amen.

Prayer Of Confession

O God, we are part of a Christian Community. We are supposed to be a caring, loving family of your sons and daughters, but there are those in our immediate family here in this fellowship, and still others in the extended family we do not know personally, who are in need. Forgive us for our lack of concern and failure to act to meet those needs. Renew a right spirit within us, and by the power of your Spirit teach us how to live in unity and harmony with one another. Amen.

Hymns

"Christ Is Alive"
"Ask Ye What Great Thing I Know"

Fourth Sunday In April

Second Lesson: 1 John 1:1—2:2
Theme: Christ Makes Known The Eternal Life

Call To Worship
At Easter Christ revealed to us the Eternal Life with the Father. This life is available to us now in the fellowship that we have with the Father and with his Son Jesus Christ.
Come, let us give thanks and praise to our Risen Lord.

Collect
From the excitement and fullness of Easter to the routine of the Sunday after — from a closeness to you to times of seeming separation — such is the pattern for many of us, O God. Come to us this morning with the refreshing power of your Spirit to rekindle in us the flame of faith. Thank you, God, for the assurance of your forgiveness and your healing touch which brings wholeness to the brokenness of life. In Jesus's name. Amen.

Prayer Of Confession
Heavenly Father, when we choose to walk in the darkness of sin we not only disrupt our relationship with you, but we rupture the bonds of fellowship that unite us with fellow Christians. We thank you for the promise of your forgiveness, Lord, and seek the power of your Spirit as we endeavor to walk in the Light that we may have fellowship with you and with one another. In Jesus' name we pray. Amen.

Hymns
"Come, Christians, Join To Sing"
"Jesus Is All The World To Me"

Fourth Sunday In April

Gospel Lesson: John 20:19-31
Theme: Through Faith You May Have Life

Call To Worship

Leader: There is one God and Father of us all, who is above all and through all and in all.
People: For all who are led by the Spirit of God are children of God.
Leader: Come, walk in the way of the Lord with songs of gladness and joy.
People: The Lord is near to all who call upon him, to all who call upon him in truth.

Collect

O Lord, we hear about people who have had miraculous experiences of your presence, but because we have not our faith in you is overshadowed by our doubts. We gather this morning that we, too, may know your living presence, receive your gracious forgiveness, and have our faith rekindled. Amen.

Prayer Of Confession

O Living Lord, we have missed out on so much in life because we have faltered when we were supposed to be following you. Strengthen our faith and help us to find that full life that awaits those who believe that you are the Son of God in whose name we pray. Amen.

Hymns

"Beams Of Heaven As I Go"
"My Faith Looks Up To Thee"

First Sunday In May

First Lesson: Acts 3:12-19
Theme: The Power Of Faith In The Risen Christ

Call To Worship

Leader: O God, answer us when we pray.
People: Be kind to us, and hear our prayers.
Leader: Remember that the Lord has chosen the righteous for his own.
People: He hears us when we call to him.

Collect

Lord, we are often surprised by your goodness and mercy. We see lives transformed, people freed from the bonds of illness that plague their bodies, minds, and souls, and we wonder whose power or godliness made it possible. We gather this morning to hear once again the message that faith in the Risen Christ makes all things new, and that if we repent of our sins, spiritual strength will be ours. Amen.

Prayer Of Confession

O God, when we are swayed by the crowd to put our faith in material things we lose sight of our need for that spiritual strength and renewal that comes only from faith in your Son, Jesus Christ. By your Spirit may that faith be ours, directing our every action and leading us into lives of service. Amen.

Hymns

"Hymn Of Promise"
"Precious Lord, Take My Hand"

First Sunday In May

Second Lesson: 1 John 3:1-7
Theme: Children Of God

Call To Worship
We are created in God's image!
We are the children of God.
If children, then heirs, joint heirs with Christ.
Come, let us give thanks to the Father, and sing praises to his holy name!

Collect
Almighty God, our Father, we your children delight in your love, and stand in awe before the gift of your Son, Jesus Christ, who has freed us from the burdens of our sins. Make us worthy of your faith in us that by the power of your Spirit and our faith in Christ we may show our love for you through acts of love and mercy to those we meet day by day. Amen.

Prayer Of Confession
Father, we are not worthy to be called your children for we have not always lived in union with Christ. With this prayer of repentance we offer ourselves anew to be your faithful children with the help and power of your Holy Spirit. Through Jesus Christ, our Lord and Savior. Amen.

Hymns
"Children Of The Heavenly Father"
"O God In Heaven"

First Sunday In May

Gospel Lesson: Luke 24:36b-48
Theme: Jesus Makes Himself Known To His Disciples

Call To Worship
You better believe it — Jesus is alive!
Because he lives we shall live also, and we are called to be witnesses to his living presence.
Come, let us worship the living Christ!

Collect
O God, grant that today as we come together to worship and pray, we may be vividly aware of your presence among us. May we sense your power and know deep within our hearts and minds the wonder of grace, peace, and love revealed through Jesus Christ our Lord. Amen.

Prayer Of Confession
Lord, we are a difficult people to convince of your living, abiding presence. Here in worship, we are keenly aware of your Spirit among us, but when we go back to our daily routine how quickly we forget. Draw us closer to you, O Living Christ, and by the power of your Spirit help us to walk with you every step of life's journey. Amen.

Hymns
"On The Day Of Resurrection"
"O Thou Who This Mysterious Bread"

Second Sunday In May

First Lesson: Acts 4:5-12
Theme: No Other Name

Call To Worship

Leader: Trust in the Lord and seek his presence.
People: Our hope is in the Lord. We gladly trust in him.
Leader: Serve the Lord with gladness for in his service we find life.
People: Since he has given us our lives, it is only just that we should serve him.

Collect

Lord, you are not only our Shepherd who restores our souls, but you are the cornerstone on which we build our lives. You are the one who saves us from our sins and gives us the hope of eternal life. In gratitude we bow before you and rededicate our lives to your service through Jesus Christ our Lord. Amen.

Prayer Of Confession

Heavenly Father, forgive us our trespasses and help us to forgive those who trespass against us. Pardon us for the times we have wandered from the right path and wandered through the darkest valleys. Restore a right spirit within us, we pray. Surely then goodness and mercy shall follow us all the days of our lives and we will dwell in your house forever. Amen.

Hymns

"Precious Name"
"All Hail The Power Of Jesus' Name"

Second Sunday In May

Second Lesson: 1 John 3:16-24
Theme: True Love Shows Itself In Action

Call To Worship
This is how we know what love is: Christ gave his life for us.

If we declare our love for Christ we must demonstrate that love with our deeds.

Come, let us worship together and hear what God has to say to us about our lives.

Collect
Lord of life and love, help us to worship you in the holiness of beauty, that some beauty of holiness may appear in us. Help us to find your will for our lives, that we may love you with our whole strength, and with glad hearts may perform those things which are pleasing to you; through Jesus Christ our Lord. Amen.

Prayer Of Confession
God of love and compassion, how often we have seen those in need, and yet have refused to help them. Forgive our selfishness, our failures to act when we could make a difference. Through your Spirit strengthen us to always and everywhere show forth your love and concern by our actions. Through Jesus Christ our Lord. Amen.

Hymns
"Where Christ And Love Prevail"
"In Christ There Is No East Or West"

Second Sunday In May

Gospel Lesson: John 10:11-18
Theme: The Good Shepherd

Call To Worship

Leader: The Good Shepherd is willing to lay down his life for his sheep.

People: Jesus is the Good Shepherd. Praise be to God!

Leader: The Good Shepherd knows his sheep and they know him.

People: Jesus is the Good Shepherd. Thanks be to God!

Leader: The Good Shepherd guides his sheep in the right paths.

People: Jesus is the Good Shepherd. His goodness and love will be with us all our lives. Hallelujah!

Collect

O Divine Shepherd, who provides for all our needs, restore our souls. Even though we walk through the darkest valley you are with us; comfort us in our sorrow. You laid down your life for us; renew our faith. You have brought us hope and given purpose to our lives through your resurrection. In this time of worship through your Holy Spirit, the love of Jesus Christ, and the comfort of your presence prepare us to follow your leading as we leave the security of this fold, and go forth to bear witness to your love. Amen.

Prayer Of Confession

O Lord, our Shepherd and our example, may we not be like the hired hand who runs away at the first sign of trouble, leaving the sheep at the mercy of those who would destroy them. Help us to follow your example as the Good Shepherd who is willing to risk and sacrifice to save the sheep. As we seek to do good and show your concern and love for others may we remember that you have other sheep that do not belong to our church or denomination. May we like the Good Samaritan be willing to minister to strangers and foreigners as well as friends and family. In Jesus' name we pray. Amen.

Hymns

"Savior, Like A Shepherd Lead Us"
"Where He Leads Me"

Third Sunday In May

First Lesson: Acts 8:26-40
Theme: Good News About Jesus Brings Joy

Call To Worship

Leader: Praise the Lord for what he has done.
People: Those who come to the Lord will praise him.
Leader: All nations will remember the Lord. From every part of the world they will turn to him.
People: The Lord is king and he rules the nations.
Leader: Future generations will speak of the Lord to the coming generations.
People: People not yet born will be told, "The Lord saved his people."

Collect

O Lord, our God, we thank you for those who shared the gospel with us and opened our hearts and minds to your saving grace. Keep us ever mindful that each generation must receive the Good News of Jesus, and they cannot understand unless it is explained by those who have found the joy of the gospel themselves. May we be instruments of that sharing through Jesus Christ our Lord. Amen.

Prayer Of Confession

Heavenly Father, we have missed many opportunities to tell others of your saving love by both word and deed. Often we have made the gospel unattractive by failing to live lives of joy and compassion. We acknowledge our responsibility for sharing the Good News about Jesus, and ask that, empowered by your Spirit, we may be used by you to bring others into the fellowship of those who put their trust in you. In Jesus' name we pray. Amen.

Hymns

"I Come With Joy"
"Come, We That Love The Lord"

Third Sunday In May

Second Lesson: 1 John 4:7-21
Theme: God Is Love

Call To Worship
God so loved the world that he gave his only Son, so that everyone who believes in him may not perish but have eternal life.
Indeed, God did not send the Son into the world to condemn the world, but in order that the world might be saved through him.
Come, let us worship the God of love.

Collect
O God of love, we give you thanks for showing your love for us by sending your Son to live among us so that we might have life through him. In gratitude we dedicate ourselves to living in ways that show forth your love for all people. We pray, too, that we may be worthy messengers so that we may be part of a world where all people learn to live together in harmony and peace as brothers and sisters. Amen.

Prayer Of Confession
God of love, we know that we should love one another, but we are quick to take offense. Retaliation is our first reaction, rather than forgiveness. Pardon our offenses, Lord, and help us to love one another even as Christ loves us. In Jesus' name we pray. Amen.

Hymns
"Sing Praise To God Who Reigns Above"
"Joyful, Joyful, We Adore Thee"

Third Sunday In May

Gospel Lesson: John 15:1-8
Theme: Stay Connected

Call To Worship

Jesus is the real vine, and we are the branches. Unless we stay connected we will wither and dry up.

Come, let us worship God, the gardener who cares for the vine and the branches!

Collect

God of all seasons, we know that in springtime our gardens need tending; we come to you that we might be pruned in order to bear fruits of the spirit that will bring a mighty harvest for your kingdom. We know that without you we can do nothing, so keep us close to you, we pray in Jesus' name. Amen.

Prayer Of Confession

Lord of the vineyard, we wish to be healthy branches bearing much fruit, but we resist the pruning that would insure a bountiful harvest. Remove from us, we pray, the suckers that would sap our strength. Keep us united to you that we may not be led astray by false promises that bear no fruit for your kingdom. In Jesus' name. Amen.

Hymns

"God Of Grace And God Of Glory"
"Blest Be The Dear Uniting Love"

Fourth Sunday In May

First Lesson: Acts 10:44-48
Theme: The Holy Spirit Is Available To All

Call To Worship

Leader: Sing for joy to the Lord, all the earth;
People: praise him with songs and shouts of joy!
Leader: Clap your hands, you rivers; you hills, sing together with joy before the Lord, because he comes to rule the earth.
People: He will rule the peoples of the world with justice and fairness.

Collect

Almighty God, our Heavenly Father, we praise you and give thanks for sending your Son, Jesus Christ, that through his life, death, and resurrection, the world might be saved. Slowly, but surely, Father, we are learning that your love extends to all who will receive it, and that there are no boundaries of nationality, race, or culture. We gather this morning as a fellowship of believers in you, bound by your Spirit with followers of Christ around the world. Praise be to you, O God. Amen.

Prayer Of Confession

Dear God, we are often surprised at those whom you welcome, and we need constantly to be reminded that your love is for everyone. Forgive our ignorance, and help us to be more outgoing in expressing our love for those you love — especially those we might easily pass by because they are different from us. In Jesus' name we pray. Amen.

Hymns

"Come Down, O Love Divine"
"Like The Murmur Of The Dove's Song"

Fourth Sunday In May

Second Lesson: 1 John 5:1-6
Theme: Faith Conquers The World

Call To Worship
Leader: Friends, hear the Good News! You are part of God's family.
People: Our love for God means that we obey his commands.
Leader: God's commands are not a burden, but a delight to those who love the Lord.
People: Our God has given us dominion over his creation, and we will deal wisely and responsibly with his world.

Collect
Heavenly Father, we take time out this morning from our struggles to overcome the pressures of the world to renew our faith in you and the power of your Spirit. Be with us in our worship that, feeling your presence, we may know that we are not alone, and go forth to face the trials and temptations of the week ahead secure in the knowledge that by our faith in you we can win the victory over the world. This we pray in the name of Jesus, Son of God. Amen.

Prayer Of Confession
O Lord, you have created us to be your children in a world that needs our witness to your love. Forgive us when we allow our pride to blind us to the fact that all persons are your children. Help us humbly to serve your kingdom as forgiven sinners who hold out to other sinners the promise of your forgiving love. Amen.

Hymns
"We've A Story To Tell To The Nations"
"Pass It On"

Fourth Sunday In May

Gospel Lesson: John 15:9-17
Theme: Friends Of God

Call To Worship

Leader: A friend is kind and ready to help, one whom we trust and respect.

People: We choose our friends; they are not forced upon us.

Leader: A friend is approachable, supportive — one in whom we can confide.

People: We esteem our friends and feel warmth and affection for them.

All: Let us be friends to one another.

Collect

Heavenly Father, your Son has taught us that the greatest love one can have for friends is to give one's life for them. Jesus showed this love by going to the cross for us. We would show our love for you, O God, by committing our lives to obeying your will for us. Through this time of worship may we be better prepared to serve you by serving others, and thus show forth your love for all your children. In Jesus's name we pray. Amen.

Prayer Of Confession

O God, Jesus called his followers "friends." We would be worthy of that honor and pray that with the help of your Spirit we may love one another even as you love us. Help us to live up to the responsibilities of friendship with each other and with you. In Jesus' name. Amen.

Hymns

"All Praise To Our Redeeming Lord"
"What A Friend We Have In Jesus"

First Sunday In June

First Lesson: Acts 1:1-11
Theme: The Promise Of The Holy Spirit

Call To Worship

We seek God's kingdom. It is right that we should come together to worship God, our creator, sustainer, and hope; but do not tarry too long gazing into the heavens with anticipation. We are called to receive the power of the Holy Spirit and then to bear witness to that heavenly kingdom which is available beginning now.

Come, let us prepare ourselves as disciples of our Lord and Savior.

Collect

O God, we join the cries that have come down through the ages asking: "When, Lord, will your kingdom come?" We realize it is not for us to know, but we thank you for the promise that you do not leave us alone, you are with us, and your Spirit will empower us as we work for your kingdom. For this we are grateful. Amen.

Prayer Of Confession

As we wait impatiently for a future kingdom, remind us again, Lord, that Jesus taught us the kingdom of God is within us. Open our hearts to let you rule our lives that we may show forth your love, and thus lead others into that glorious realm where you reign. Amen.

Hymns

"The Voice Of God Is Calling"
"Jesus, Thine All-Victorious Love"

First Sunday In June

Second Lesson: Ephesians 1:15-23
Theme: Christ Set Free To Be The Head Of The Church Universal

Call To Worship
Leader: Lift up your hearts.
People: We lift them up unto the Lord.
Leader: Let us worship and give thanks unto him.
People: He is the way, the truth, and the life, both now and forever.

Collect
O God, on this day when we mark the Ascension of our Lord, we give you thanks for Jesus's life on earth and also for his ascension into glory where he is now free to be with all his followers everywhere and at all times. Help us in this time of worship to become more keenly aware of what it means for him to be the Head of the Church Universal, and for each of us as a part of that body. We pray in Jesus' name. Amen.

Prayer Of Confession
Lord Jesus Christ, we have faith that your power working in us is the same as God used in raising you from the dead to be the living head of the church. Forgive us when we fail to use that power to further your kingdom, and to be your body in the world by showing forth your love. In Jesus' name we pray. Amen.

Hymns
"Open My Eyes, That I May See"
"All My Hope Is Firmly Grounded"

97

First Sunday In June

Gospel Lesson: Luke 24:44-53
Theme: Jesus' Departure Brought Joy

Call To Worship

Leader: Worship the Lord with joy; come before him with happy songs.

People: We acknowledge that the Lord is God. He made us and we belong to him.

Leader: Enter the Temple gates with thanksgiving, and its courts with praise.

People: We give thanks to him and praise him.

Leader: The Lord is good; his love is eternal.

People: And his faithfulness lasts forever.

Collect

Lord, like those early disciples we rejoice at your Ascension. We give thanks constantly to God for your life among us and for your eternal presence through all ages. We await your power that will enable us to be your faithful witnesses to all peoples everywhere. Amen.

Prayer Of Confession

Lord, we have taken your message of repentance and forgiveness of sins very personally, and we give you thanks for the hope and promise of new life which it brings to us. Now we understand that this message is not just for a select group, but it is to be preached to all nations. Your promise of power that will enable us to be your messengers brings us great joy. Thanks be to God. Amen.

Hymns

"Crown Him With Many Crowns"
"Hail, Thou Once Despised Jesus"

Second Sunday In June

First Lesson: Acts 2:1-21 or Ezekiel 37:1-14
Theme: The Spirit Brings Life

Call To Worship

Leader: O Lord, how manifold are your works.
People: **In wisdom you have made them all: the earth is full of your creatures.**
Leader: May the glory of the Lord endure forever; may the Lord rejoice in his works.
People: **I will sing to the Lord as long as I live; I will sing praise to my God while I have being.**
Leader: May my meditation be pleasing to him, for I rejoice in the Lord.
People: **Bless the Lord, O my soul. Praise the Lord!**

Collect

O Lord, on that first Pentecost you breathed new life into your disciples and changed them from listless and disillusioned men and women into enthusiastic, excited, and exuberant witnesses to your power. May your Spirit so fill us this day that we, too, may take on a new dedication and devotion to the work of your kingdom, through the same Holy Spirit. Amen.

Prayer Of Confession

Lord, we wander aimlessly in a barren land, flesh and bones going listlessly about our daily tasks, without purpose or meaning. There is no life in us. Open our hearts and minds to your Spirit that we might receive real life and find direction and energy to fulfill your purpose for us. In Jesus' name. Amen.

Hymns

"See How Great A Flame Aspires"
"O Breath Of Life"

Second Sunday In June

Second Lesson: Acts 2:1-21 or Romans 8:22-27
Theme: The Coming Of The Holy Spirit

Call To Worship

Leader: God says, "This is what I will do in the last days: I will pour out my Spirit on everyone."

People: "Your sons and daughters will proclaim my message, your young shall see visions, and your elderly shall dream dreams."

Leader: And there appeared to them tongues as of fire which rested on each of them.

People: All of them were filled with the Holy Spirit.

Collect

Almighty God, today we celebrate the outpouring of your Holy Spirit onto believers at Pentecost, bringing them together in unity of purpose as your Body in the world. Give us that same Spirit, we pray, so that the fires of enthusiasm may be lit among us and within us as we work together to carry out your mission in the world. As ambassadors of Christ may we live power-filled lives that show forth your love and your concern for everyone. We pray in the name of Jesus Christ, the head of the Church, our Savior. Amen.

Prayer Of Confession

Lord, your disciples waited patiently in Jerusalem for the coming of your promised power to carry out their mission. Forgive our impatience which is often due to our blindness in not recognizing the coming of your Spirit, and our failures to use the power you have given us. Let the wind of your Spirit blow upon us and once again fan the flames of your power in us. Amen.

Hymns

"O Spirit Of The Living God"
"O Thou Who Camest From Above"

Second Sunday In June

Gospel Lesson: John 15:26-27; 16:4b-15
Theme: The Work Of The Spirit

Call To Worship

God's love has been poured into our hearts through the Holy Spirit which has been given to us.
The Holy Spirit reveals the truth about God and his Son, Jesus Christ.
Come, let us worship God the Father, Son, and Holy Spirit.

Collect

Lord, just as the early disciples did not at first recognize Jesus after his resurrection, so, too, we do not always recognize you, God, as our understanding of you matures. Thank you for the gift of your Holy Spirit that opens our eyes to the Truth that frees us from childhood concepts and enables us to witness to your far-reaching and ever-present love for all humanity. Amen.

Prayer Of Confession

O God, many times we are confused about what is right and what is wrong. We try to make decisions on our own even though we have the Helper, the Advocate, the Counselor available to guide us. Forgive our foolish self-reliance, Lord, and help us to reach out to your Holy Spirit to show us your way. In Jesus' name. Amen.

Hymns

"Filled With The Spirit"
"Of All The Spirit's Gifts To Me"

Third Sunday In June

First Lesson: Isaiah 6:1-8
Theme: Who Will Go?

Call To Worship
Leader: Holy, holy, holy is the Lord of hosts;
People: the whole earth is full of his glory.
Leader: Holy, holy, holy is the Lord God Almighty who was and is
and is to come.
**People: O Lord God, great and mighty is your holy name, and to
you we ascribe all honor and glory, Father, Son, and Holy
Spirit.**

Collect
Glory be to you, Lord God Almighty! You have revealed yourself
to us as Father, Son, and Holy Spirit. Through your Son Jesus Christ,
as well as the Holy Spirit, we have come to know your love for us and
for all your creation. In this time of worship open our ears to hear your
call to be messengers of your love, and give us the courage to respond: "Here am I, send me." Amen.

Prayer Of Confession
Lord, we have heard you calling, but have turned a deaf ear to
your pleading. Grab our attention, we pray, and help us to respond to
your forgiveness with repentance and a readiness to do your will. In
Jesus' name we pray. Amen.

Hymns
"Come, Thou Almighty King"
"Lord, Whose Love Through Humble Service"

Third Sunday In June

Second Lesson: Romans 8:12-17
Theme: God's Children

Call To Worship

Leader: Those who are led by God's Spirit are God's children.
People: **Since we are his children, we will possess the blessings he keeps for his people.**
Leader: The Spirit that God has given you does not make you afraid; instead the Spirit makes you God's children.
People: **By the Spirit's power we cry out to God, "Father, my father."**

Collect

Almighty God, we would worship you as Father, Son, and Holy Spirit. We are grateful to be called your children and to have the love of our Heavenly Father. We are awed by the sacrifice of your Son, Jesus Christ, through which we have known your forgiveness and promise of eternal life. In our joys and in our sorrows your Holy Spirit has counseled and comforted us with power to remain steadfast in our loyalty to you. We come now to give you praise and glory as we seek your continuing care and listen for your word of challenge. Amen.

Prayer Of Confession

O God, we seek to avoid anything that causes us suffering and pain. May we hear again the challenge of your word not to live as our human nature wants us to, but by the Spirit. Strengthen us that we may stand up for what your Spirit tells us is right even if it involves suffering. Show us how to share Christ's suffering that we may also share his glory. Amen.

Hymns

"Every Time I Feel The Spirit"
"God The Spirit, Guide, And Guardian"

Third Sunday In June

Gospel Lesson: John 3:1-17
Theme: Christ Came To Save The World

Call To Worship

We do not worship a vengeful God who is out to destroy us.

God is love, and he sacrificed his Son that the world might be saved through him.

God sent his Holy Spirit to empower us to carry on Jesus's ministry of salvation.

Come, let us worship God Almighty, Father, Son, and Holy Spirit.

Collect

Heavenly Father, we know that when they crucified your Son, Jesus Christ, you did not leave us comfortless. You sent your Holy Spirit to show us that through Christ and your Spirit you are always with us. In the faith and hope of an eternity with you we strive to do your will and to witness to your forgiving love, that your kingdom may come and your will be done on earth as it is in heaven. Amen.

Prayer Of Confession

Sometimes, Lord, we think it is impossible to change our old ways. Then we hear your Spirit saying to us that we must be born again. We realize we cannot be the old self and the new person in Christ at the same time, so we come to you seeking that new life in Christ that comes when we surrender all. Come into our lives, Lord, and give us new life. We pray in Jesus's name. Amen.

Hymns

"Holy, Holy, Holy! Lord God Almighty"
"Christ For The World We Sing"

Fourth Sunday In June

First Lesson: 1 Samuel 17:(1a, 4-11, 19-23) 32-49
Theme: The Giants Who Would Enslave Us

Call To Worship

Leader: The Lord rules the world with righteousness;
People: he judges the nations with justice.
Leader: The Lord is a refuge for the oppressed,
People: a place of safety in times of trouble.
Leader: Those who know you, Lord, will trust you;
People: you do not abandon anyone who comes to you.

Collect

Heavenly Father, we are truly thankful for the many blessings you have given us. In your strength we have made it through difficult days. But in spite of your goodness to us we still cry out for help. We face many giants that would enslave us, and under our own power we are not able to overcome them. We pray for your Holy Spirit to give us the help we need to stand up to these Goliaths such as greed, jealousy, prejudice, and so many others. Be close to us, God. By your strength we know that we can be more than conquerors through Jesus Christ our Lord. Amen.

Prayer Of Confession

Heavenly Father, you have sent us on the simple errand of taking food to your sons and daughters, and we have failed to see the larger task of doing battle against the Goliaths of greed and ignorance that cause so much of the world's hunger. Open our eyes to these larger needs, and gird us for the battle with your Spirit of love, caring, and concern. In Jesus' name. Amen.

Hymns

"Onward, Christian Soldiers"
"A Mighty Fortress Is Our God"

Fourth Sunday In June

Second Lesson: 2 Corinthians 6:1-13
Theme: Weapons Of Righteousness

Call To Worship

Leader: Listen! Today is the day to be saved! This is the hour to receive God's call.

People: We will answer when he calls. We will go where he sends us.

Leader: We have righteousness as our weapon when we serve God!

People: We will seek to know his will so that we can share him with everyone.

Collect

O God, once again we gather together to acknowledge you as our heavenly Father, and to see your blessing and guidance. Help us, then, to learn to be still and listen to you. May we hear the Good News of your unconditional love offered to us in Jesus Christ. May we hear your invitation to accept Jesus as our Lord and Savior, and thus discover the fullness of life in his abiding presence. Amen.

Prayer Of Confession

Eternal God, we want to be counted among your faithful disciples, but we are unwilling to inconvenience ourselves or our friends. We tolerate blatant injustices, saying and doing only enough to quiet our consciences. Lord, forgive our pettiness and our feeble attempts to serve you. Give us the courage to take a stand for righteousness, regardless of the personal cost, so that we may be found worthy of you and deserving of your grace. Amen.

Hymns

"We'll Understand It Better By And By"
"How Like A Gentle Spirit"

106

Fourth Sunday In June

Gospel Lesson: Mark 4:35-41
Theme: Why Are You Afraid?

Call To Worship

Leader: Come to the Lord, whose love can dispel all our worries and fears.

People: Even though we trust in the Lord, we still face the future afraid of the storms life brings.

Leader: Commit yourself completely to the care of our loving God. Only then will your faith be greater than your fears.

People: Come into our hearts, Lord. Abide with us and turn our fears into fearlessness.

Collect

Almighty God, Creator of the universe, reassure us that the inner storms of our own nature are not beyond your control, your quieting touch, so that we may trust you more fully and find the calm we need when circumstances threaten to swamp us. In Jesus' name. Amen.

Prayer Of Confession

When the storms of life come up unexpectedly, Lord, we are afraid they will be our undoing. The winds are too strong, the waves too high, we are sure that we will perish and we are afraid. We cry out to you, O God, and we hear you say: "Be quiet, be still, peace!" Grant us that peace in all our days; strengthen our faith and our courage; and send us out as courageous messengers of that peace. Amen.

Hymns

"Lonely The Boat"
"Jesus, Savior, Pilot Me"

Fifth Sunday In June

First Lesson: 1 Samuel 1:1, 17-27
Theme: The Loss Of A Friend

Call To Worship

Leader: From the depths of my despair I call to you, Lord.
People: Hear my cry, O Lord; listen to my call for help!
Leader: I wait eagerly for the Lord's help, and in his word I trust.
People: I wait for the Lord more eagerly than sentries wait for the dawn.
Leader: Trust in the Lord, because his love is constant and he is always willing to save.
People: He will save his people from all their sins.

Collect

Almighty God, our Heavenly Father, thank you for this opportunity of sharing together in worship. It is good that we come apart from the routine of daily life to be part of a fellowship where we need not be lonely, where we can reach out in love to one another without fear of being rejected.

Guide us in our worship, O God, that our lives may be enriched, and that we may be empowered to be your people. In Jesus' name we pray. Amen.

Prayer Of Confession

O Lord, forgive us for our indifference when things are going well, and our demanding prayers when things go wrong. Pardon us for accepting our many blessings but failing to assume the responsibility of being a blessing to others. We pray in Jesus' name. Amen.

Hymns

"There Is A Balm In Gilead"
"How Firm A Foundation"

Fifth Sunday In June

Second Lesson: 2 Corinthians 8:7-15
Theme: Testing Our Love

Call To Worship

Leader: Come, let us worship God with our whole being, holding nothing back.

People: It is difficult to go so far as to give ourselves, our money, our talents, but we will try.

Leader: God will fill our hearts, if we will open them to his presence.

People: Here we are, Lord. Fill us with your divine love.

Collect

Lord, we have great plans for what we can do to further your kingdom. As we come to this time of worship we pray that your Spirit will come upon us and make us as eager to finish the plan as we were to make it. In this way, O God, we can show how real our love for you is. Amen.

Prayer Of Confession

Lord, you have blessed us in so many ways, and often we are tempted to think that we deserve all that we have, that it is some sort of reward for our good deeds. Forgive us, we pray, and help us to see that since we have plenty it is only fair that we should help those in need. Grant us your spirit of love and generosity and caring. We pray in Jesus' name. Amen.

Hymns

"More Love To Thee, O Christ"
"Breathe On Me, Breath Of God"

Fifth Sunday In June

Gospel Lesson: Mark 5:21-43
Theme: The Power Of Faith

Call To Worship

Leader: Come before the Lord with all your needs, all you who are heavy laden.

People: In his presence we find the strength to go on when we have thought we were finished.

Leader: Nothing can bring us so low that his presence cannot bring us hope.

People: We trust in him. We have faith in his power to give us new life.

Collect

Lord, we come before you with many burdens. They are too heavy for us to carry alone, so we come seeking your strength and renewed courage from your Holy Spirit. Take control of our lives and give us new life that we may serve you all of our days. Amen.

Prayer Of Confession

Lord Jesus, we know that through the Holy Spirit you are always with us, but when serious illness or the death of loved ones confront us, we still feel so all alone. Be especially near us in our time of deepest need, Lord, and open our hearts to an awareness of your comforting, strengthening, renewing presence. We pray in Jesus' name. Amen.

Hymns

"Faith, While Trees Are Still In Blossom"
"Lift Every Voice And Sing"

First Sunday In July

First Lesson: 1 Samuel 5:1-5, 9-10
Theme: The Call To Leadership

Call To Worship
Leader: The Lord is great
People: and is to be highly praised.
Leader: We have heard what God has done,
People: and now we have seen it.
Leader: This God is our God forever and ever.
People: He will lead us for all time to come.

Collect
Almighty God, how great you are. You have blessed us beyond measure, and given each of us gifts that would enable us to serve you by ministering to your children. We come this morning with open minds and hearts seeking your will for our lives and asking your help in discovering those talents and skills we have allowed to lie dormant. Through your Holy Spirit may we not only acknowledge these gifts but also have the courage and determination to use them in accordance with your will. Amen.

Prayer Of Confession
O Lord, we confess that hidden talents serve no purpose in your kingdom. Forgive our shyness, our reticence, our unwillingness to trust you, and make us willing to be faithful stewards of that which has been entrusted to our care. In Jesus' name we pray. Amen.

Hymns
"Freely, Freely"
"We Are Climbing Jacob's Ladder"

First Sunday In July

Second Lesson: 2 Corinthians 12:2-10
Theme: God's Grace Is All You Need

Call To Worship

Just as we all have strengths we should be sharing, so, too, we all have weaknesses. When we are able to deal with those thorns in the flesh by the power of God's grace, that, too, we need to share.

Come, and in our worship may we discover anew God's grace that makes us strong.

Collect

Eternal God, your presence enables us to carry on when we are beset by trials that threaten to undo us. Armed with your love, we find that the rough places are made plain, and we are able to walk in newness of life. May all people praise you and find your presence in their lives. We pray in Jesus' name. Amen.

Prayer Of Confession

O God, remove from us all self-pity. Keep us from whining and complaining about our weaknesses or our frailty. Make us indeed as new creatures who have overcome our shortcomings, and substituted the things we can do for those we no longer are able to do. Help us to see those gifts you have given us that we may be filled with patience and hope that will enable us to be realistic about our abilities. Amen.

Hymns

"Praise To The Lord, The Almighty"
"Rise, Shine, You People"

First Sunday In July

Gospel Lesson: Mark 6:1-13
Theme: Dealing With Rejection

Call To Worship

It is frustrating to witness to God's love, and to be rejected. We worship a God who understands how we feel because he has been there, too. Nevertheless his message to us is one of hope and determination. Come, let us worship the God of hope!

Collect

Lord, when our neighbors and especially our own families do not respond when we witness to your love, keep us from discouragement. In this time of worship revitalize our faith. Help us to renew our determination to be your witnesses and to leave the results in your hands. Amen.

Prayer Of Confession

Sometimes, Lord, when we are rejected we tend to become argumentative, belligerent, demanding, and emotional. Infuse us with your Holy Spirit that we may never stop loving, and help us to accept rejection as we move on to other opportunities. In Jesus' name. Amen.

Hymns

"O Young And Fearless Prophet"
"God Will Take Care Of You"

Second Sunday In July

First Lesson: 2 Samuel 6:1-5, 12b-19
Theme: Dancing For The Lord

Call To Worship

Leader: The world and all that is in it belongs to the Lord.
People: The earth and all who live on it are his.
Leader: Who has the right to enter the Lord's holy Temple?
People: Those who are pure in act and in thought.
All: The Lord will bless them and save them.

Collect

O Lord, our God, we honor you and praise your holy name. We lift our voices in songs of praise, and our music expresses our joy. Your goodness and mercy fill our whole being, and our bodies express our gratitude to you as we dance with all our might to honor you. May our worship today be a celebration of your goodness toward us, and may we be exuberant in our joy. Amen.

Prayer Of Confession

Lord, help us to give our whole selves to you without holding anything back. Even in our stillness may we dance before you as an expression of our total commitment to your Son, Jesus Christ, our Savior. Amen.

Hymns

"Lord Of The Dance"
"Joy To The World"

Second Sunday In July

Second Lesson: Ephesians 1:3-14
Theme: Spiritual Blessings In Christ

Call To Worship

Leader: Fling wide the gates, open the ancient doors.
People: And the great king will come in.
Leader: Who is this great king?
People: He is the Lord, strong and mighty; the Lord, victorious in battle.
Leader: Fling wide the gates, open the ancient doors.
People: And the great king will come in.
Leader: Who is this great king?
People: The triumphant Lord — he is the great king!

Collect

Almighty God, Father of our Lord Jesus Christ, and our Father, too, we give you thanks. You have given us every spiritual blessing, and through the sacrifice of your Son our sins are forgiven and we are set free. We come now to praise your glory and to seek your power as we strive to bring all persons together with Christ as our head. Amen.

Prayer Of Confession

God, we know that it was because of your love that you decided that through Jesus Christ you would make us your children. We often forget that we love you because you first loved us. Make us truly grateful, Lord, and strengthen our desire to be your faithful children. In Jesus' name we pray. Amen.

Hymns

"Sent Forth By God's Blessing"
"Shalom To You"

Second Sunday In July

Gospel Lesson: Mark 6:14-29
Theme: Misused Power

Call To Worship

Leader: The Lord reigns; let the earth rejoice.
People: **I will be glad and exult in you, I will sing praise to your name, O Most High.**
Leader: Yours, O Lord, is the greatness, and the power, and the glory, and the victory, and the majesty, for everything that is in the heavens and in the earth is yours; yours is the kingdom, O Lord, and you are exalted as head above all.
People: **Because your steadfast love is better than life, my lips will praise you.**

Collect

O Lord, we praise your name and acknowledge your power. Help us to know the power you have given us through your Holy Spirit, that we may use it wisely, justly, and with mercy and love. Keep us from abusing our power by using it for selfish ends or to increase our own power without subjecting it to your will. We pray in Jesus' name. Amen.

Prayer Of Confession

Lord, little do we realize the consequences of our grudges, our hurt feelings, our desire for revenge. Cleanse our hearts, we pray, that we may be free to live in accordance with your will. We pray in Jesus' name. Amen.

Hymns

"For All The Saints"
"Your Love, O God"

Third Sunday In July

First Lesson: 2 Samuel 7:1-14a
Theme: God's Dynasty Continues Forever

Call To Worship

Leader: Come, people of vision and dreams. Come to the Lord and see if your plans are God's plans.

People: We come before the Lord. Open our eyes and our hearts that we may be sure we are doing God's will.

Leader: Seek wisdom, O servants of God, for without wisdom all visions are empty and useless.

People: Open our eyes and our minds, O Lord, so that we may understand what we see.

Collect

O God, we have listened to words of encouragement from those who have said we can do whatever we have in mind because the Lord is with us. In our wiser moments we know that this is backward, and so we come before you seeking to know what you have in mind for us. May this time of worship be an occasion for us to respond: "Your will be done." Amen.

Prayer Of Confession

Lord, we are often so confident that you are with us that we do whatever we have in mind expecting you to rescue us if things don't go as planned. Fill us with your Holy Spirit that we may have the wisdom to lay our plans before you prior to going ahead with them. In this way may we truly know that we are following your will and not just our own. Amen.

Hymns

"God Of The Ages"
"O Worship The King"

Third Sunday In July

Second Lesson: Ephesians 2:11-22
Theme: We Are All One In Christ

Call To Worship

Leader: Christ has broken down the walls of hostility that have separated us and kept us enemies with other peoples and races.
People: By means of the cross Christ has united us into one body.
All: It is through Christ that all of us are able to come in the one Spirit into the presence of the Father.

Collect

Father in heaven, when we try to segregate other peoples, races, and nations, it is we who are being kept apart from you. We give you thanks that the walls of hostility have been broken down, and that in Christ we recognize that we are all part of the family of God. May this time of worship be a time when we recommit ourselves to Christ, through whom we are all able to come in the one Spirit into your holy presence. Amen.

Prayer Of Confession

Almighty God, if there are walls of animosity, jealousy, and prejudice that separate us from one another and from you, help us to see where we have had a part in erecting them. Then by the power of your Spirit give us the courage to take the initiative in tearing them down. In Jesus' name we pray. Amen.

Hymns

"O Church Of God United"
"In Christ There Is No East Or West"

Third Sunday In July

Gospel Lesson: Mark 6:30-34, 53-56
Theme: Do Not Grow Weary In Well-Doing

Call To Worship
Even when we come apart to worship and find respite from the troubles of the world, we will find among us those who stand in need of being ministered to. They are those for whom our touch and words of encouragement will provide the strength and healing they need.

Come, let us worship together, and let us be sensitive to each other's needs.

Collect
O God, even as Jesus sought to get away with his disciples from the clamoring crowds, so we, too, seek the peace and quiet that comes from withdrawal from our busy weekday schedules. Lord, even as Jesus found there was no escape from the needs of people, so may we also realize the need to be ever alert to where we can serve and worship you best by ministering to others. Through Jesus Christ our Lord, we pray. Amen.

Prayer Of Confession
Heavenly Father, when we are tempted to pass by on the other side because we are anxious to meet our own needs, help us to have compassion for those by the wayside who need our help. We pray in Jesus' name. Amen.

Hymns
"Jesus' Hands Were Kind Hands"
"Where Cross The Crowded Ways Of Life"

Fourth Sunday In July

First Lesson: 2 Samuel 11:1-15
Theme: When Our Leaders Fail Us

Call To Worship

Leader: Be still, so God may speak to you in the silence of your heart.

People: O Lord, we need your peace, there is so little in the world.

Leader: Seek God's peace, and you will find it. Share it and you will be blessed.

People: Lord, we are ready to receive your peace, and to spread love throughout the land.

Collect

Lord, when we are tempted to waver from our ideals, we look to the power of your Spirit to keep us on the right path. Help us, we pray, to improve the way we live. Through Jesus Christ our Lord. Amen.

Prayer Of Confession

O God, not only do we fail to follow your commandments, but when we stray we scheme at the expense of others to cover up our wrongdoing. We ask for your forgiveness, Lord, and pray that despite our shortcomings we may still be found useful in your service. Amen.

Hymns

"What Does The Lord Require?"
"O God Of Every Nation"

Fourth Sunday In July

Second Lesson: Ephesians 3:14-21
Theme: The Love Of Christ

Call To Worship

Leader: Come and bow before our Heavenly Father, from whom every family in heaven and on earth takes its name.

People: We pray that we may be strengthened in our inner being with power through the Spirit.

Leader: To him who by the power at work within us is able to accomplish abundantly far more than all we can ask or imagine;

People: to him be glory in the Church and in Christ Jesus to all generations, forever and ever. Amen.

Collect

Almighty God, our Heavenly Father, we praise you and give you thanks for the gift of your Son, Jesus Christ. It is through him that we have come to know your boundless love for all your children. As we worship you this day we open our hearts in faith, and pray that Christ will make his home there. Amen.

Prayer Of Confession

O Lord, our faith is weak and our knowledge of you is so limited that we can't possibly know the breadth and length and height and depth of your love. Grant us your Spirit, we pray, that we may have the power to comprehend, and that we may be completely filled with the very nature of God. Through Jesus Christ our Savior. Amen.

Hymns

"The Church's One Foundation"
"My Jesus, I Love Thee"

Fourth Sunday In July

Gospel Lesson: John 6:1-21
Theme: When We Offer All That We Have To God

Call To Worship
The disciples were baffled by the problem of how to feed the thousands until they offered all that they had to Jesus.

In our day and age, thousands, if not millions, are facing hunger of body and soul. God is calling for our total commitment to caring and sharing.

Come, let us worship the God of mercy who needs us to carry out his ministry.

Collect
Heavenly Father, you have blessed us and provided for our needs. Now we would be your body providing for the needs of others. Challenge us in this time of worship and show us what miracles can happen when we make a total commitment to you. In Jesus' name. Amen.

Prayer Of Confession
When we are confronted with problems that overwhelm us, Lord, we are tempted to give up and say: "It can't be done." Help us, we pray, to have faith in your power, and then grant us vision to look for new ways to solve old problems. Through Jesus Christ, our Lord. Amen.

Hymns
"Close To Thee"
"Come, Thou Fount Of Every Blessing"

First Sunday In August

First Lesson: 2 Samuel 11:26—12:13a
Theme: Accepting Responsibility For Our Failures

Call To Worship

Leader: Create in me a pure heart, O God,
People: and put a new and loyal spirit in me.
Leader: Give me again the joy that comes from your salvation,
People: and make me willing to obey you.

Collect

O God, as we draw near to you in worship help us to see ourselves as others see us. We have done many foolish things just to satisfy our own desires. We need your loving forgiveness and your Spirit within us to overcome our selfish ways. Come into our hearts, Lord Jesus, come. Amen.

Prayer Of Confession

Heavenly Father, we have no one to blame for our failure to keep your commands. In your great mercy forgive our mistakes, confront us with the truth about ourselves, and help us once again to get on the right path. In Jesus' name we pray. Amen.

Hymns

"All People That On Earth Do Dwell"
"Softly And Tenderly Jesus Is Calling"

First Sunday In August

Second Lesson: Ephesians 4:1-16
Theme: The Unity Of The Body

Call To Worship

Leader: I am the Church, you are the Church.

People: We are the Church together.

Leader: When we are children we think only of ourselves. When we mature we are supposed to put aside childish ways.

People: We must grow up in every way to Christ, who is the head of the Church.

All: There is one God and Father of all people. Come, let us worship together in a spirit of unity.

Collect

Lord, we come together in a spirit of unity. Speak to each of us that we may realize our particular gifts, and prepare us to use them to build up the Church as Christ's body on earth. We pray in Jesus' name. Amen.

Prayer Of Confession

O God, often we have been blown about by every shifting wind of teaching, as some new religious fad sweeps across our path. Help us to grow up to Christ, and stand firm in his teaching that all his children are needed for the Church, his body on earth, in order fully to carry out his mission. Keep us from all pride and prejudice that prevent us from accepting others who may differ from us, but who share our faith and our knowledge of the Son of God. Amen.

Hymns

"Awake, O Sleeper"
"Many Gifts, One Spirit"

First Sunday In August

Gospel Lesson: John 6:24-35
Theme: The Bread Of Life

Call To Worship
We come seeking the Bread of Life — the food that lasts for eternal life. Jesus said, "I am the Bread of Life. Those who come to me will never be hungry."
Come, all you who are hungry for the Bread of Life, and let us worship together.

Collect
Almighty God, we know that we do not live by bread alone, and so we come seeking that Spiritual Bread that can sustain and nourish our whole selves. As we seek you in this time apart from the demands of the world, may we feast on that eternal bread found in your Son, Jesus Christ our Lord. Amen.

Prayer Of Confession
Lord, how foolish we have been. Our spirits have been starving for nourishment, and yet we have refused the Bread of Life which is ours simply by turning to you. Open our hearts and minds that accepting you we may gain new life and vitality, now and always. Amen.

Hymns
"You Satisfy The Hungry Heart"
"O Food To Pilgrims Given"

Second Sunday In August

First Lesson: 2 Samuel 18:5-9, 15, 31-33
Theme: Would That I Could Have Died In Your Place

Call To Worship

How tragic it is to lose someone you love.

The forlorn cry of the one left behind rings in our ears: "I would gladly have died in your place, my love."

Come, let us worship the God of Comfort, remembering that his only Son, Jesus Christ, died for us.

Collect

Heavenly Father, we pray for all those who have lost sons and daughters, and particularly those who died prematurely under tragic circumstances. Send the comfort of your Holy Spirit; walk with them in their sorrow as one who has gone through this suffering, and help them to find the strength to go on living. In Jesus' name we pray. Amen.

Prayer Of Confession

Almighty God, in life's darkest hours we feel so all alone — deserted by family and friends, yes, even by you, Lord. Then out of the depths we cry to you, and we wait for you. We know that our hope is in you, and that with you there is steadfast love and great power to redeem. Amen.

Hymns

"O Love Divine, What Hast Thou Done"
"How Great Thou Art"

Second Sunday In August

Second Lesson: Ephesians 4:25—5:2
Theme: Characteristics Of Our New Life

Call To Worship

Leader: From the depths of our despair we call to you, Lord.
People: Hear my cry, O Lord, listen to my call for help.
Leader: If you kept a record of our sins, who could escape being condemned.
People: But you forgive us, so that we should stand in awe of you.

Collect

O God, we would have our lives controlled by your love. Our aim is to be kind and tenderhearted to one another, and to forgive one another, as you have forgiven us through Christ. We need your strength and guidance as we come to give you thanks and praise your holy name. Amen.

Prayer Of Confession

O God, our tongues run away from us, and we find ourselves using harmful rather than helpful words. When we should be building one another up, we blurt out hurtful words that tear down. Forgive us, Lord, and through your Holy Spirit teach us so that what we say will do good to those who hear us. Amen.

Hymns

"Spirit Song"
"Are Ye Able"

Second Sunday In August

Gospel Lesson: John 6:35, 41-51
Theme: The Promise Of Eternal Life

Call To Worship

Leader: Friends, why have you come?
People: We gather in the name of Jesus Christ, our Lord.
Leader: What are you doing here?
People: We come seeking the Bread of Life, to reaffirm our claim to eternal life, and to be renewed.
Leader: Will you open your ears, your eyes, your hearts to the Lord?
People: We will receive what God has for us in this hour.

Collect

O God, as we come to you this day hungering and thirsting for your word, so feed us with the Bread of Life that we may sense the renewing power of your Spirit, and begin to live with a new awareness of your love and purpose for each of us. In the life-giving name of Jesus we pray. Amen.

Prayer Of Confession

Lord, we thank you for the new life you have given us that enables us to enter your kingdom now and for all eternity. We confess that we find it difficult always to love the way Jesus taught. With grateful hearts we claim the forgiveness you have promised, and seek the power of your Holy Spirit to show forth your love in all our words and deeds. In Jesus' name we pray. Amen.

Hymns

"The King Of Love My Shepherd Is"
"How Blest Are They Who Trust In Christ"

Third Sunday In August

First Lesson: 1 Kings 2:10-12; 3:3-14
Theme: Seek Wisdom

Call To Worship

Leader: The way to become wise is to honor the Lord;
People: he gives sound judgment to all who obey his commands.
All: He is to be praised forever.

Collect

Lord, like Solomon of old we, too, pray for wisdom to know the difference between good and evil. You have blessed us in many ways, and we are grateful. We want to please you and walk in your ways, but we are weak and need your help. Grant us this wisdom, we pray, in Jesus' name. Amen.

Prayer Of Confession

O God, we pray for wisdom, but then we lack the determination and self-discipline to pursue it. Help us, Lord, to grow in wisdom by prayer, study, and worship even as your Son did, in whose name we pray. Amen.

Hymns

"God Of Grace And God Of Glory"
"Immortal, Invisible, God Only Wise"

Third Sunday In August

Second Lesson: Ephesians 5:15-20
Theme: Living As Wise People

Call To Worship

Leader: With all my heart I will thank the Lord.

People: How wonderful are the things the Lord does!

Leader: The Lord is full of honor and majesty; his righteousness is eternal.

People: In all he does he is faithful and just; all his commands are dependable.

Collect

We come to you this morning, Lord, to give you thanks and praise. We know that these are troublesome times because your voice goes unheeded, and we live like ignorant people ignoring your commands. Enlighten us by your Holy Spirit that we might know your will. By the same Holy Spirit light a fire within us that we may go forth to testify to your love. We pray in the name of our Lord, Jesus Christ. Amen.

Prayer Of Confession

Heavenly Father, we have wasted a great deal of time when we should have been serving you. We are not lazy, just thoughtless and irresponsible. Grant us the wisdom we need, Lord, to know your will and to do it. Amen.

Hymns

"Spirit Of The Living God"
"Be Thou My Vision"

Third Sunday In August

Gospel Lesson: John 6:51-58
Theme: The Bread Of Eternal Life

Call To Worship

Leader: What are you doing here?
People: **We have come searching for the key to eternal life.**
Leader: Jesus said: "I am the living bread. If you eat this bread you will live forever."
People: **How can we eat Jesus?**
Leader: Accept the fact that Jesus died to bring us the love of God, and God raised him from death to life to show us that the Spirit is eternal.
People: **We would let Jesus into our lives. Thanks be to God!**

Collect

Praise be to you, O God, for the gift of your Son, for the promise of eternal life, and for the indwelling Spirit of your love. Help us to live as those who have taken on the life of Christ that we might demonstrate your love to the world. Amen.

Prayer Of Confession

O God, help us to love you more fully, to serve you more eagerly, and to worship you more sincerely. Too often the world turns away from you because of what they see in us who call ourselves by your name. Forgive us, Lord, and enable us to demonstrate your light and your love in all that we do. Amen.

Hymns

"O The Depth Of Love Divine"
"Deck Thyself, My Soul, With Gladness"

Fourth Sunday In August

First Lesson: 1 Kings 8:(1, 6, 10-11) 22-30, 41-43
Theme: Pray That All The Peoples Of Earth May Know God

Call To Worship

Leader: With my whole being I sing for joy to the living God.

People: How happy are those whose strength comes from you.

Leader: The Lord is our protector and glorious king, blessing us with kindness and honor.

People: He does not refuse any good things to those who do what is right.

All: Lord Almighty, how happy are those who trust in you.

Collect

Lord, we know that you are not confined to our sanctuary, and that you are not our exclusive God but the God of all creation. We give you thanks for the assurance that there is no place we can hide from you or escape from your love. Use us, we pray, that all the peoples of the world may know you and obey you. We pray in Jesus' name. Amen.

Prayer Of Confession

God Almighty, our Father, we like to think we have a special place in your plans, and that we have an exclusive place in your heart. Help us, Lord, to recognize and accept that your love extends to all people everywhere. Use us to show your love without regard to race, nationality, or religious background. Amen.

Hymns

"O God Of Every Nation"
"This Is My Song"

Fourth Sunday In August

Second Lesson: Ephesians 6:10-20
Theme: Be Prepared

Call To Worship
Which of you preparing to do battle against the forces of evil in the world would not first sit down and count the cost? We are gathered here in the house of God to prepare ourselves to combat the wrongs in our society. As we worship our Lord, let us check the armor that God gives us, so that when we leave we will be able to take a stand for peace, justice, truth, and harmony among all God's children.

Collect
O Lord God Almighty, grant us wisdom, grant us courage for the facing of this hour. Clothe us with truth, righteousness, faith, salvation, and your Word that we may be able to stand up against evil and announce to the world the Good News of peace. Amen.

Prayer Of Confession
O God, when love and mercy seem to be defeated by hate and vengeance, may our faith in you and your ultimate triumph never waiver. Help us to keep alert, and may we always speak boldly to share the Good News of your love made known to us through Jesus Christ our Lord. Amen.

Hymns
"Soldiers Of Christ Arise"
"Standing On The Promises"

Fourth Sunday In August

Gospel Lesson: John 6:56-69
Theme: Bread Of Heaven

Call To Worship

Leader: Let us worship God with songs of praise and prayers of thanksgiving.

People: His presence fills our hearts to overflowing.

Leader: Let us worship God with our lives, serving him wherever he calls us.

People: His love is so great we have to share it. It is too good to keep for ourselves.

Collect

O Lord, we have gathered here this morning that our spiritual bodies may be nourished by the Bread of Life. We know, Lord, that you have the words of eternal life, and we open our hearts and minds to receive your word for you are the Holy One who has come from God. Amen.

Prayer Of Confession

O God, when we read the Scriptures and try to take the words literally we find ourselves confused. The parables, metaphors, and symbols move us to disbelief. Open our eyes and minds to the truths the words convey, and give us a better understanding of your message for us today. We pray in Jesus' name. Amen.

Hymns

"Become To Us The Living Bread"
"Holy Spirit, Truth Divine"

Fifth Sunday In August

First Lesson: Song of Solomon 2:8-13
Theme: A Time For Singing

Call To Worship

Leader: Come, let us thank the Lord for his steadfast love,
People: and for his wonderful works to those who love him.

Collect

Lord, we thank you for every sign of your abiding love. Everywhere we look we see signs of your amazing creation. We glory in the gift of your Son, Jesus Christ, who has demonstrated your love for us. Yes, this is a time for singing, and we raise our voices in praise of you. Amen.

Prayer Of Confession

O God, with every passing season you come to us and invite us to go with you that we might come to know your love. You never cease loving us even though we do not deserve it. In this time of worship let us seize the opportunity to respond to your call by saying: "Yes, we will go with you!" Amen.

Hymns

"Let's Sing Unto The Lord"
"Morning Has Broken"

Fifth Sunday In August

Second Lesson: James 1:17-27
Theme: Hearing And Doing

Call To Worship
Do any of you think you are religious? If so, do not deceive yourselves by just listening to God's word; instead, put it into practice.

Come, and as we worship let us listen for God's word. Let us prepare ourselves to go from this place and put it into practice.

Collect
Almighty God, by your Holy Spirit take control of our lives. May our actions show to the world that your love abides in us and through us. We do not wish to pay lip service only to your commands, but to be loyal participants in the work of your kingdom. Thanks be to you, O God. Amen.

Prayer Of Confession
Lord, we confess that we are often quick to speak and slow to listen. We are ready with a quick retort when we should be trying to understand what is troubling others. Forgive our quick tempers, we pray, and help us to become good listeners, ready to seek reconciliation and eager to show forth your love. Amen.

Hymns
"Lord, Whose Love Through Humble Service"
"Forth In Thy Name, O Lord"

Fifth Sunday In August

Gospel Lesson: Mark 7:1-8, 14-15, 21-23
Theme: Evil Ideas Lead To Immoral Deeds

Call To Worship
When we break God's commands we are often quick to blame outer circumstances. Let us come before the Lord this morning ready to take responsibility for our actions, and seeking a pure heart.

Collect
Heavenly Father, we, your children, need your help. O Creator God, we come asking you to create in us clean hearts. We know that the evil that is in us shows up in our greed, deceit, jealousy, slander, pride, and folly. By your Spirit establish your love in our hearts that it may shine in our every word and action. Amen.

Prayer Of Confession
Lord, we are prone to judge ourselves and make decisions based on what is acceptable in society. Wake us up, Merciful God, to the freedom you have given us from customs and conformity that we may follow your will and only your will in deciding what is good and right and pleasing to you. Amen.

Hymns
"I Want A Principle Within"
"Lord, I Want To Be A Christian"

First Sunday In September

First Lesson: Proverbs 22:1-2, 8-9, 22-23
Theme: The Lord Made Us All

Call To Worship

Leader: Serve the Lord with a right spirit.

People: What is the right spirit in serving God?

Leader: A spirit of loving service to others, which seeks not self-glory, but benefit for those you serve.

People: We will give of ourselves in service to God and to his people.

Collect

Almighty God, our Maker, Creator of rich and poor alike, through our worship may we be inspired to renew our commitment to serve you by serving others. Open our eyes to the needs of those who are hungry that we may diligently seek to show our compassion by our deeds. In Jesus' name. Amen.

Prayer Of Confession

Lord, when did we see you hungry and not feed you, thirsty and not give you a drink? We know the answer all too well, Lord, and we beg your forgiveness. By the power of your Holy Spirit, Lord, enable us to seek out those in need and minister to them in your name. Amen.

Hymns

"For The Beauty Of The Earth"
"This Is My Father's World"

Fifth Sunday In September

Second Lesson: James 2:1-10 (11-13), 14-17
Theme: Actions Prove Our Faith

Call To Worship

Leader: If we would find God in our lives, if our worship is to be fulfilling, we must seek God's will for us.

People: **Speak to us, Lord, as we open our ears and our hearts to your presence in our lives.**

Leader: The Lord is present to those who seek him in a spirit of love and humility.

People: **We place our lives in your hands, O Lord. Lead us and we will follow.**

Collect

Lord, we your children are gathered in your house to give you thanks and praise. We come from many different walks of life, but with the knowledge that we are all equal in your sight, and that you show no favorites. In that spirit we come, too, to renew our vow to love you with heart, mind, soul, and strength, and to love our neighbors as ourselves. In the name of Christ we pray. Amen.

Prayer Of Confession

O God, despite our best intentions we find ourselves discriminating against some of our neighbors for a variety of reasons. When our actions or lack of actions belie our faith, we need your forgiveness. Send your Holy Spirit upon us that we may truly serve you by doing all that we possibly can to meet the needs of our neighbors. For Christ's sake. Amen.

Hymns

"O Church Of God United"
"Here, O Lord, Your Servants Gather"

139

First Sunday In September

Gospel Lesson: Mark 7:24-37
Theme: The Power Of Faith Is Not Limited

Call To Worship
As we worship let us draw near to Jesus who has the power to make us whole. Let us keep our eyes on Jesus on whom our faith depends from beginning to end.

Collect
Divine Physician, we would draw near to you in this time of worship, for we know that you can make us whole. We thank you for your sensitivity to and awareness of the needs of others. You care for people, the hungry and the oppressed. You restore sight and help the stooped to stand tall. You give new heart to the bereaved and hopeless. Our faith is in you and we know you will not disappoint us. Amen.

Prayer Of Confession
O Gracious God, you created us for fellowship with you and so that we might serve you by making rough places plain, making this a better world for your children. We have often failed in this task, even after you sent Christ to free us from the sins which bound us fast. We still prefer the snug harbor of our sins to the open seas of life where problems often seem overwhelming. Forgive us for our fears, Lord, and grant us the courage that cares enough to give of our very best in service to you and to our world. Amen.

Hymns
"Faith Of Our Fathers"
"O Master, Let Me Walk With Thee"

Second Sunday In September

First Lesson: Proverbs 1:20-33
Theme: Wisdom Calls

Call To Worship

Leader: The law of the Lord is perfect; it gives new strength.
People: **The commands of the Lord are trustworthy, giving wisdom to those who lack it.**
Leader: The laws of the Lord are right, and those who obey them are happy.
People: **The commands of the Lord are just and give understanding to the mind.**
All: **May my words and my thoughts be acceptable to you, O Lord, my refuge and my redeemer.**

Collect

Lord, we ask your blessing upon us as we gather to give thanks for all your goodness toward us. Open our ears and hearts to hear the voice of Wisdom calling us. Help us to discern your Truth that we may be led by your Spirit into paths of greater service. Amen.

Prayer Of Confession

Merciful God, we confess that we have ignored your advice and have not been willing to listen to your correction. Pour out your Holy Spirit upon us that we may gain a heart of wisdom, and set our feet upon a straight path that we may serve you with heart, mind, soul, and strength. Amen.

Hymns

"Open My Eyes, That I May See"
"Dear Jesus, In Whose Life I See"

Second Sunday In September

Second Lesson: James 3:1-12
Theme: Taming The Tongue

Call To Worship
Leader: Reverence for the Lord is good;
People: it will continue forever.
Leader: The judgments of the Lord are just;
People: they are always fair.
Leader: None of us can see our errors;
People: deliver me, Lord, from hidden faults!
All: May my words and my thoughts be acceptable to you, O Lord, my refuge and my redeemer.

Collect
O Lord, our God, how wonderful are your works throughout the earth. We have come together to praise you and give thanks for your many blessings. May the words that come from our mouths come also from our hearts that we may truly show our thanks by the lives we live. In Jesus' name we pray. Amen.

Prayer Of Confession
O God, how sorrowful we are when we reflect on the times when we have let loose our unbridled tongues in words that have stampeded us into turmoil and run rampant over the feelings of others. Forgive us, we pray, and through your Holy Spirit enable us to control our tongues. Amen.

Hymns
"Just As I Am, Without One Plea"
"Lord, Speak To Me"

Second Sunday In September

Gospel Lesson: Mark 8:27-38
Theme: The Cost Of Discipleship

Call To Worship
Come, let us worship the Lord by responding to his invitation. Leave self behind, take up your cross, and follow Jesus. Walk in the Lord's presence in the land of the living. Come!

Collect
Almighty God, who suffers with us when we must endure pain, and has shown us through your Son, Jesus Christ, who suffered the pain of death upon the cross, that you are always with us, grant us courage to accept suffering as well as healing and help, for your name's sake. Give us inner strength by your Spirit, that we may be faithful in the confession of your name, Jesus Christ, Son of the living God. Amen.

Prayer Of Confession
God and Father of us all, you are the source of life and love, and we join our voices in praise. We thank you for the call which has come to each of us today: "Come, follow me." Forgive us for we have heard but failed to respond. Help us to be sensitive to the message of your love revealed in Jesus Christ, and help us to respond by taking up our cross and following you. Amen.

Hymns
"Take Up Thy Cross"
"Where He Leads Me"

Third Sunday In September

First Lesson: Proverbs 31:10-31
Theme: True Happiness

Call To Worship

Leader: Happy are those who reject the advice of evil people,
People: who do not follow the example of sinners or join those who have no use for God.
Leader: Instead, they find joy in obeying the law of the Lord,
People: and they study it day and night.
Leader: They are like trees that grow beside a stream,
People: that bear fruit at the right time, and whose leaves do not dry up.

Collect

Almighty God, our Creator and Redeemer, like your children everywhere we are caught up in the pursuit of happiness. There are those who urge us to find it in seeking wealth, and others who claim it can be found by being ambitious and seeking self-glorification. We come to worship you this morning because we believe true happiness can only be found in following your commands and serving you. Bless our worship, we pray, in Jesus' name. Amen.

Prayer Of Confession

Lord, we want to serve you in a manner that could be rated among the best, but when we look at the attributes of one who serves her family best, we realize we fall far short. We are not as generous to the poor and needy as we could be. We often fear for the future. We do not always speak with a gentle wisdom, and in many other ways we need to improve. Strengthen us in our resolve to be better servants of our Lord, we pray in Jesus' name. Amen.

Hymns

"For The Beauty Of The Earth"
"O Happy Day, That Fixed My Choice"

Third Sunday In September

Second Lesson: James 3:13—4:3, 7-8a
Theme: Draw Near To God And He Will Draw Near To You

Call To Worship

We come together to worship Almighty God who alone can give us the wisdom and understanding we need to produce a harvest of good deeds free from prejudice and hypocrisy.
Come, draw near to God, and he will draw near to you.

Collect

We draw near to you, O God, in the expectation that the Holy Spirit will bring us into communion with you. We confess Jesus to be our champion against the power of evil and seek his power to resist all evil in and around us. In his name we pray. Amen.

Prayer Of Confession

Lord, we confess that in our weakness, jealousy, bitterness, and selfishness sometimes seem to get the upper hand. Even though it leads to quarreling and disorder, we find it hard to overcome. We seek your forgiveness, Lord, and ask that through your Holy Spirit we may overcome these temptations and receive the wisdom from above that is pure, peace-loving, considerate, and open to reason. Amen.

Hymns

"Near To The Heart Of God"
"Nearer, My God To Thee"

Third Sunday In September

Gospel Lesson: Mark 9:30-37
Theme: Who Is The Greatest?

Call To Worship

Jesus said: "Let the children come to me, and do not stop them, because the kingdom of God belongs to such as these."

Jesus said: "Whoever welcomes in my name one of these children, welcomes me, and whoever welcomes me, welcomes not only me but also the one who sent me."

Come, let us worship the Father who reminds us of our responsibility to welcome the children with enthusiasm, with respect, and with the open arms of the heart.

Collect

Christ who walked among us in human form and walks with us still in the indwelling Spirit, teach us the greatness that is expressed by the embrace of a child, rather than by rubbing shoulders with the rich and powerful, so that we may serve in the manner of your servanthood. Amen.

Prayer Of Confession

Lord, when we try to measure greatness we usually pass over the children, assuming that they are out of the running. We forget that Jesus taught us to embrace them, for to such belongs the kingdom of God. Open our eyes and our hearts, Lord, that we may come to understand that in your eyes all are precious, all may find wisdom and true greatness. We ask it in Jesus' name. Amen.

Hymns

"Tell Me The Stories Of Jesus"
"Children Of The Heavenly Father"

Fourth Sunday In September

First Lesson: Esther 7:1-6, 9-10; 9:20-22
Theme: Speak Up For Freedom

Call To Worship

Leader: How shall we serve our God who has blessed us in so many ways?

People: We serve him best by serving those of his children who stand in dire need, particularly those who are oppressed and denied freedom of thought.

Leader: Let us praise the Lord with our lips and our lives, walking in the way of holiness and love.

People: Thank you, God, for giving us the greatest gift, the chance to serve you and yours.

Collect

God of mercy, look upon your children who are kept prisoners by abuse, poverty, and discrimination. May we never remain silent when our voice can be lifted on their behalf.

May this time of worship provide us with the inspiration, the motivation, and the insight to act on their behalf. We ask in Jesus' name. Amen.

Prayer Of Confession

Heavenly Father, forgive us for the times when our own welfare has kept us from taking action that would carry out your will. Forgive us for the times we have expressed love with our lips but have denied it by the way we live our lives. Forgive us for the times we were sure of your will, but only did what pleased us. Renew a right spirit within us, Lord, and free us to do your will. In the name of Jesus Christ we pray. Amen.

Hymns

"Where Cross The Crowded Ways Of Life"
"Lift Every Voice And Sing"

147

Fourth Sunday In September

Second Lesson: James 5:13-20
Theme: The Prayer Of Faith

Call To Worship
Let us thank the Lord who has not let our enemies destroy us.

Those enemies could be sickness, sorrow, selfishness, suspicion, anger, anxiety, arrogance, or a host of other enemies of the soul.

Come, let us worship the Lord who made heaven and earth and from whom our help comes!

Collect
Lord, in the face of many trials and troubles that besiege us we often feel helpless and alone. Remind us once again that the Scriptures counsel those who are in trouble to pray, and that all of us in the fellowship of the Church are to pray for others. Renew our faith in the power of prayer and in your eternal presence. We ask in Jesus' name. Amen.

Prayer Of Confession
Heavenly Father, we confess that we have often felt powerless in the face of need because we couldn't figure out a solution to the problem. Forgive us, we pray, and keep us ever mindful of the power of prayer and faith that solutions come from you, Almighty God. Amen.

Hymns
"Sweet Hour Of Prayer"
"This Is My Song"

Fourth Sunday In September

Gospel Lesson: Mark 9:38-50
Theme: Not Everyone Who Serves The Lord Belongs To Our
Denomination

Call To Worship

Leader: Worship the Lord with joy.
People: We come before him with happy songs!
Leader: Acknowledge that the Lord is God.
People: He made us and we belong to him.
Leader: The Lord is good; his love is eternal.
People: His faithfulness lasts forever.

Collect

O Lord and Master of us all, set our hearts on fire with the desire
to know your will, and send us among your people to serve them in
love. Free us from fear so that the Good News of Jesus may reach the
world through us without hurt or hindrance. Give us hearts full of
love, eyes to see the needs of others, and hands open to help. In your
precious name we pray. Amen.

Prayer Of Confession

Heavenly Father, we confess that there are times when our faith
waivers, doubts beset us, and we are hindered in our desire to serve
you and you alone. By the power of your Spirit enable us to cut ourselves free from all such obstacles that we may have the salt of friendship, and live at peace with one another. For Christ's sake we pray.
Amen.

Hymns

"I Love Thy Kingdom, Lord"
"Jesus Shall Reign"

First Sunday In October

First Lesson: Job 1:1; 2:1-10
Theme: Testing Our Faith

Call To Worship

Leader: Examine me and test me, Lord; judge my desires and thoughts.

People: Your constant love is my guide; your faithfulness always leads me.

Leader: Lord, I wash my hands to show that I am innocent and march in worship around your altar.

People: I sing a hymn of thanksgiving and tell all your wonderful deeds.

Leader: Do not destroy me, O Lord, with the sinners; spare me from the fate of those who do evil all the time.

People: As for me, I do what is right; be merciful to me and save me.

Collect

Lord, we are quick to sing your praises when good things happen to us. We try not to complain when trouble comes. We know that you are always with us to give us the strength we need to endure the bad times, and to resist the temptations that come with the good. Praise be to you, O God! Amen.

Prayer Of Confession

Lord, in our weaker moments we sometimes wonder if it really pays to be good. So often, as we look around us, evil seems to triumph. Then your spirit comes upon us; our hope and faith in your final triumph are renewed; and we move forward with joy because we know we are on the right side. In Jesus' name we offer this prayer. Amen.

Hymns

"Leaning On The Everlasting Arms"
"I Will Trust In The Lord"

First Sunday In October

Second Lesson: Hebrews 1:1-4; 2:5-12
Theme: The One Who Leads Us To Salvation

Call To Worship
In the past God has spoken to us through the prophets, and more recently through his Son who came to dwell among humans. Today he still speaks to us through the prophets, his Son Jesus Christ, and through the Holy Spirit. As we gather to worship let our hearts and minds be open to hear God speak.

Collect
Heavenly Father, you have brought us together as your visible body in Christ that we might hear your word. Through this time of worship may each one of us find our commission. Make our fellowship rich, we pray, with all your saints on earth and in heaven; through Jesus Christ our Lord. Amen.

Prayer Of Confession
O God, what are human beings that you should think of them, mere human beings that you should care for them? Yet you have made them a little lower than the angels, and made them to rule over all things. Forgive us, we pray, when we have been unworthy of such trust, and enable us by your Spirit to accept our responsibility as your children and joint heirs with Christ of your kingdom. Amen.

Hymns
"'Tis So Sweet To Trust In Jesus"
"I Know Whom I Have Believed"

First Sunday In October

Gospel Lesson: Mark 10:2-16
Theme: Jesus Teaches About The Family

Call To Worship
Come, let us worship God who calls us to have faith in him with the trust of a little child. Let us lift our voices in praise and thanksgiving to God who has given us an example of true love through his Son, Jesus Christ.

Collect
Lord, within our families we come to know something of your love. Here we know the love that brings us together, as well as the love that sometimes requires forgiveness and fresh starts. In our families we learn the faith and trust of little children and strive to follow their example. Help us, Lord, as we strive to make our families even more a haven of love, encouraging one another in our spiritual growth. We pray in Jesus' name. Amen.

Prayer Of Confession
Help us, Father, to let this time of worship bring to each of us a new beginning for a life which would leave behind all that is negative and critical, and to move forward in the power of your love into a life which becomes positive and reaffirming, through Jesus Christ our Lord. Amen.

Hymns
"Jesus Loves Me"
"When Love Is Found"

Second Sunday In October

First Lesson: Job 23:1-6, 16-17
Theme: Where Is God When We Need Him?

Call To Worship
In our despair we cry out: "My God, my God, why have you abandoned me?"

In faith and trust we remember the words of Jesus: "Ask and you will receive, seek and you will find, knock and the door will be opened to you."

Come, and as we worship our faith will be renewed!

Collect
O Lord, revive our spirits, renew our trust, and help us to see when we have looked for you in the wrong places, as well as when we have expected the answers to our prayers to be on our schedule. Grant us the calm that can be still and know that you are God, and the power that enables us to ride out the storm and find the good in everything. In Jesus' name. Amen.

Prayer Of Confession
Forgive us, Lord, for the gloom and negative attitude which often control our thoughts and actions. May we know and share enthusiastically the power of your love to transform the negative into the positive. In Jesus' name. Amen.

Hymns
"Stand By Me"
"I Want Jesus To Walk With Me"

Second Sunday In October

Second Lesson: Hebrews 4:12-16
Theme: Jesus, The Great High Priest

Call To Worship
Through Jesus Christ who lived among us, was tempted as we are, knew sorrow and discouragement, betrayal, and cruel death — God knows and understands how we feel. As we worship let us come before the Lord, from whom nothing is hidden, and receive his forgiveness, mercy, and love. Come!

Collect
O God, we come together once again to worship you with praise and thanksgiving. We have been through another week, and our experiences have been different. Nevertheless, we come with our common need of forgiveness, acceptance, and love. May we truly hear your reassuring words of life; may we respond to the touch of your healing power of love; and may we become channels of that life-giving love as we live our daily lives. In Jesus' name we pray. Amen.

Prayer Of Confession
O God, we know that you judge the desires and thoughts of our hearts, and that there is nothing that can be hid from you. Cleanse the desires and thoughts of our hearts, we pray, and create in us a pure spirit, wholly acceptable to you. Amen.

Hymns
"Jesus, Lover Of My Soul"
"O Love That Wilt Not Let Me Go"

Second Sunday In October

Gospel Lesson: Mark 10:17-31
Theme: The Price Of Eternal Life

Call To Worship
Leader: To you, O Lord, I offer my prayer;
People: in you, my God, I trust.
Leader: Teach me your ways, O Lord;
People: make them known to me.
Leader: Teach me to live according to your truth,
People: for you are my God, who saves me.

Collect
Eternal God, through your Son, Jesus Christ, we have been promised eternal life. Jesus also taught that we cannot earn eternal life simply by obeying your commandments. In our worship this day, help us to see that eternal life is a gift from you, Father. What is required of us is total commitment to you, and that we do what is just, show constant love, and live in humble fellowship with you. Let your Holy Spirit dwell within us that we may be your faithful children throughout our journey through life. Amen.

Prayer Of Confession
Lord, we often find it difficult to give up our possessions. In our search for the good life we get mixed up in our priorities. Forgive us, we pray, and help us to get straight in our thinking that we may always seek first your kingdom. In Jesus' name we pray. Amen.

Hymns
"Amazing Grace"
"Let Us Plead For Faith Alone"

155

Third Sunday In October

First Lesson: Job 38:1-7 (34-41)
Theme: Do You Have All The Answers?

Call To Worship

Leader: Praise the Lord, my soul! O Lord, my God, how great you are!

People: You are clothed with majesty and glory; you cover yourself with light!

Leader: Lord, you have made so many things!

People: How wisely you made them all!

Leader: I will sing to the Lord all my life;

People: as long as I live I will sing praises to my God.

All: Praise the Lord, my soul!

Collect

O God, Creator and Sustainer of the universe, the best minds in our scientific community keep probing the depths of your creation trying to answer the questions you put to Job. Each generation adds to our knowledge, yet only adds emphasis to what we already know. How marvelous is your creation; how wonderful are the works of your hands. We gaze at the heavens through our powerful telescopes and ask again: "What are human beings that you are mindful of them?"

In our worship draw near to us, God, and as we humble ourselves in your presence, make us keenly aware of our responsibility as stewards of your creation. Amen.

Prayer Of Confession

Lord, we acknowledge that sometimes we act as if we know it all, when in truth we know very little. Forgive our arrogance and grant us wisdom. Draw us nearer to Christ that through him we may grow daily in our understanding and knowledge of you, Almighty God. In Jesus' name we pray. Amen.

Hymns

"Holy God, We Praise Thy Name"
"All Things Bright And Beautiful"

Third Sunday In October

Second Lesson: Hebrews 5:1-10
Theme: The Source Of Eternal Salvation

Call To Worship

Leader: Let us test and examine our ways, and return to the Lord!
People: **Let us lift up our hearts to God.**
Leader: With what shall I come before the Lord, and bow myself before God on high?
People: **He has showed you what is good; and what does the Lord require of you but to do justice and to love kindness, and to walk humbly with your God.**

Collect

O God, when we cry for help in time of trouble, you answer us in love. As we hear your word and sing your praise may we enjoy the fullness of salvation by the Most High, through your lowly Son, Jesus Christ, our Lord and the source of our eternal salvation. Amen.

Prayer Of Confession

O God, no one likes to suffer, and we are no exception. Without the power of your Holy Spirit we could not endure it, but with your help we have faith that even though it is unpleasant we can walk through the valley of the shadow of death. Help us to go beyond endurance when suffering comes, to the point where we can use it to learn valuable lessons. We pray in Jesus' name. Amen.

Hymns

"Ask Ye What Great Thing I Know"
"Trust And Obey"

Third Sunday In October

Gospel Lesson: Mark 10:35-45
Theme: True Greatness

Call To Worship

Do you expect the seat of honor at a banquet?
Do you volunteer for the sake of recognition?
Do you go the extra mile in your place of employment looking for a raise or promotion?
Come, let us worship our God, and learn what he has to say about "greatness."

Collect

Almighty God, we come seeking your wisdom. Frankly, there are still some things we don't fully understand — such as: "the last shall be first," "lose your life in order to find it," "to be great you must be a servant." Enlighten us, Lord, and by your Spirit enable us to be faithful followers of your way. Amen.

Prayer Of Confession

Heavenly Father, we get our values and priorities mixed up. We seek success rather than opportunities for service. We expect others to recognize us rather than our being quick to see the needs of others. You can straighten us out, Lord, by the working of your Holy Spirit. Come and take control of our lives, we pray, in Jesus' name. Amen.

Hymns

"Guide Me, O Thou Great Jehovah"
"Ye Servants Of God"

Fourth Sunday In October

First Lesson: Job 42:1-6, 10-17
Theme: Job Perseveres And Finds New Life

Call To Worship
Leader: I will always thank the Lord; I will never stop praising him.
People: I will praise him for what he has done; may all who are oppressed listen and be glad!
Leader: Proclaim with me the Lord's greatness;
People: let us praise his name together.

Collect
O God, we thank you for your patience with us as we struggle to keep our faith in you even as we face life's trials and tribulations. Like a loving parent you persist with us until at last we see for ourselves the right direction our lives should go. Then in your bountiful goodness you give us new life. Thanks be to you, Heavenly Father. Amen.

Prayer Of Confession
Lord, you call us to follow you, and we are willing as long as you lead us through green pastures and beside still waters. However, when the trail leads through fields covered with thorns or across raging rivers, our courage fails, and we hold back. Forgive us, Lord, and help us to realize that today is the day we are to follow you no matter what lies ahead. Amen.

Hymns
"I Need Thee Every Hour"
"Close To Thee"

Fourth Sunday In October

Second Lesson: Hebrews 7:23-28
Theme: Jesus, Our High Priest Forever

Call To Worship

Leader: I prayed to the Lord, and he answered me;
People: he freed me from all my fears.
Leader: The oppressed look to him and are glad;
People: they will never be disappointed.
Leader: The helpless call to him, and he answers;
People: he saves them from all their troubles.

Collect

Good Lord, you are more than fair; you are merciful. You are not stingy but generous in your blessings bestowed on us. You are more than approachable; you are loving and outgoing. We do not love you as we ought, but we do love you. Accept our love and help us to love you more. Amen.

Prayer Of Confession

Lord, we are so thankful that we have an advocate with the Father, even Jesus Christ, your Son and our High Priest. It costs so little to be kind, and yet that seems too much for us. We are unwilling to take the time or go out of our way to help our neighbor. Forgive us, we pray, for your great mercy's sake, and help us break the cycle of our busyness so we can stop long enough to see the opportunities for serving you that confront us daily. Amen.

Hymns

"O God In Heaven"
"Standing On The Promises"

Fourth Sunday In October

Gospel Lesson: Mark 10:46-52
Theme: Faith With Action Brings New Vision

Call To Worship
Leader: The righteous call to the Lord, and he listens;
People: he rescues them from all their troubles.
Leader: The Lord is near to those who are discouraged;
People: he saves those who have lost all hope.
Leader: Good people suffer many troubles,
People: but the Lord saves them from them all.

Collect
Almighty God, in times of weakness as well as strength, in times of darkness as well as light, you have blessed us. Grant, our Father, that this may be a new day for each one of us. Heal the blindness of our spirits that we may have a new vision of our calling and a new awareness of our purpose. Give to us the vision to see where you go before us on life's road that we may follow you more closely and serve you by serving others. May we discover those deep inner resources of love made available to us in Jesus Christ, our Lord and Savior. Amen.

Prayer Of Confession
O God, we find life closing in on us. We do not know what the future holds and we are afraid. We are blinded by the cries of the world to satisfy our own desires, and we find it difficult to see the road you would have us travel. We know that you can help us to see more clearly, and so we pray that you will give us new insight and a new determination to follow you. In Jesus' name we pray. Amen.

Hymns
"I Heard The Voice Of Jesus Say"
"God Of Our Life"

First Sunday In November

First Lesson: Ruth 1:1-18
Theme: Faithfulness

Call To Worship

Leader: Praise the Lord! Praise the Lord, O my soul!

People: I will praise the Lord as long as I live. I will sing praises to my God all my life long.

Leader: Happy are those whose hope is in the Lord their God,

People: who made heaven and earth, the sea, and all that is in them.

Leader: The Lord lifts up those who are bowed down.

People: He protects the strangers who live in our land; he helps widows and orphans.

All: Let all God's creatures praise his holy name forever.

Collect

O Lord, if we did not have faith in your abiding presence and listen for your guidance we could not face the future. So much happens in our lives: the untimely death of loved ones, the disruption of moving to strange places, changes in our economic status. We could go on and on, Lord, but you know how it is. Through it all we put our trust in you. Help us to live fully in the present moment — letting the past be the past, and trusting in your presence as we move into the future. Give us the power of hope which will enable us to keep on keeping on. In Jesus' name we pray. Amen.

Prayer Of Confession

Merciful Father, we do not come here pretending we are better than other folks. Rather, we gather here because we know that we can never save ourselves. We know that we can be forgiven only by your grace. We are weak in ourselves, and need the power of your Holy Spirit. Therefore, we come seeking your forgiveness and your power. In Jesus' name. Amen.

Hymns

"If Thou But Suffer God To Guide Thee"
"God Moves In A Mysterious Way"*

First Sunday In November

Second Lesson: Hebrews 9:11-14
Theme: Christ Cleanses Our Consciences So We Can Serve The Living God

Call To Worship

Leader: Let us praise God who sought us out while we were yet sinners.
People: His love has enabled us to take hold of life.
Leader: Let us praise God by being instruments of his will,
People: by reaching out in love to those the world is unwilling to love.

Collect

Heavenly Father, once again we have gathered in your sanctuary to share with you and one another in the spirit of your love. Let your Spirit enfold us, that we may receive new strength and experience an inner peace. Let the assurance of your forgiveness free us from guilt, enabling us to live more fully in accordance with your will and that new life which is ours in Jesus Christ. Amen.

Prayer Of Confession

Eternal God, we know that we have sinned, and our guilty conscience keeps us from living the full life. We come seeking the cleansing power of your eternal Spirit that will purify our consciences and free us so that we may serve you, the living God. This we ask in the name of Jesus Christ our Lord. Amen.

Hymns

"A Charge To Keep I Have"
"We Are Climbing Jacob's Ladder"

First Sunday In November

Gospel Lesson: Mark 12:28-34
Theme: The Great Commandment

Call To Worship

Leader: I will proclaim your greatness, God; I will thank you forever and ever.

People: The Lord is great and is to be highly praised; his greatness is beyond understanding.

Leader: People will speak of your mighty deeds and I will proclaim your greatness.

People: They will tell about all your goodness, and sing about your kindness.

Leader: The Lord is loving and merciful, slow to become angry and full of constant love.

People: He is good to everyone and has compassion on all he made.

Collect

Lord, we love you with all our being: heart, soul, mind, and strength. We come to praise you and give thanks for your many blessings. May this time of worship also be a time of renewal as we seek the power of your Spirit to enable us truly to love our neighbors as ourselves. In Jesus' name we pray. Amen.

Prayer Of Confession

Lord, we know that our love for you should show itself in the way we treat our neighbors and all with whom we come in contact, but we confess that our pride and selfishness often get in the way. We have often failed to do what we ought to have done or have done things we knew were unloving. Cleanse our hearts, we pray, with your healing presence and encourage us by your loving presence to give of our best to show forth our love for you by the love we give our neighbors. Amen.

Hymns

"Come, We That Love The Lord"
"Help Us Accept Each Other"

Second Sunday In November

First Lesson: Ruth 3:1-5; 4:13-17
Theme: Happy Ending

Call To Worship
The story of Ruth, Naomi, and Boaz is one of love, loyalty, and responsibility. As we gather together to worship God Almighty, the Father of us all, let us receive his love, renew our loyalty, and accept our responsibility for our families, loved ones, and neighbors.
Come, let us worship.

Collect
Almighty God, we give you thanks for lives set free from despair when things go wrong. Enable us to see clearly one another's needs so that we may be a ministering community. Give us strength to do your will and courage to accept our responsibility for others. We pray in Jesus' name. Amen.

Prayer Of Confession
We confess, Lord, that sometimes when we put our trust in you we use that as an excuse for doing nothing ourselves. Wake us up, we pray, that we may seek your will and then plan and strategize to carry it out. Amen.

Hymns
"Joyful, Joyful, We Adore Thee"
"God Will Take Care Of You"

Second Sunday In November

Second Lesson: Hebrews 9:24-28
Theme: Christ Takes Away Our Sins

Call To Worship

Christ died once and for all time to remove the barrier of sin that keeps us from God, and to demonstrate the forgiving and loving nature of our Heavenly Father. Christ continues to stand at the doorways of our hearts, pleading for us to let him enter and thus accept God's love.

Come, let us worship our merciful God made known to us through Jesus Christ.

Collect

O God, our help in ages past and our hope for years to come, we graciously accept your merciful and forgiving love. May your Holy Spirit inspire our prayers as we worship you in the name of Jesus Christ our Lord. Amen.

Prayer Of Confession

Good Lord, save us from halfheartedness in our service to others. May our commitment to do your will be complete, and may we find joy in the full use of all that we are and have in the service of our Savior, Jesus Christ. Amen.

Hymns

"Great Is Thy Faithfulness"
"How Like A Gentle Spirit"

Second Sunday In November

Gospel Lesson: Mark 12:38-44
Theme: Sacrificial Giving

Call To Worship

If our actions do not agree with our teachings then we are in trouble. Jesus warned us about giving out of our abundance to gain recognition, when he calls us to give sacrificially of our time, talents, and money in order to serve him.

Come, let us worship God who provides for our needs and asks us to provide for the needs of others.

Collect

Almighty God, what we give to you is nothing compared to the sacrifice of himself that Jesus made upon the cross for us. Bless this time of worship, we pray, that it may be a time when we rededicate ourselves that we may be used by you in the building of your kingdom, and in sharing the Good News of your forgiving love with those who do not know you. We pray in Jesus' name. Amen.

Prayer Of Confession

Yes, Lord, we, too, have been guilty of contributing to the work of your Church the crumbs left over after our feasting. We have not known the joy of giving because we have felt no pain in letting go such small amounts of our blessings. May your Spirit inspire us to give not what we think we can afford, but what we know in our hearts we ought to be giving for your work. Amen.

Hymns

"Take My Life, And Let It Be"
"I Would Be True"

Third Sunday In November

First Lesson: 1 Samuel 1:4-20
Theme: Hannah's Prayer

Call To Worship

Leader: You, Lord, are all I have, and you give me all I need;
People: how wonderful are your gifts to me; how good they are!
Leader: I praise the Lord, because he guides me.
People: I am always aware of the Lord's presence; he is near and nothing can shake me.
Leader: And so I am thankful and glad, and I feel completely secure.
People: I have served you faithfully, and you will not abandon me.

Collect

Lord, we are desperate when our prayers seem to go unanswered. We come together this morning to give thanks and sing your praises. We are a diverse group with a wide variety of concerns, but we know that you are aware of each of our needs. Hear our petitions, O Lord, and help us to give ourselves in service to you. We pray in Jesus' name. Amen.

Prayer Of Confession

God and Father of us all, we come into your presence in the spirit of expectancy. In faith we believe that you are here with us and you will speak to us. May each of us experience the fulfillment of that promise. May we learn to be still, to listen for your word, and then be responsive to your call through Jesus Christ, our Lord and Savior. Amen.

Hymns

"Sweet Hour of Prayer"
"Prayer Is The Soul's Sincere Desire"

Third Sunday In November

Second Lesson: Hebrews 10:11-14 (15-18), 19-25
Theme: A Call To Persevere

Call To Worship
Let us come near to God with a sincere heart and a sure faith, with hearts that have been purified from a guilty conscience.
Come, let us worship together!

Collect
Heavenly Father, we come together as part of your body on earth realizing that we need each other. By ourselves we are weak and limited in what we can accomplish. Together and led by your Spirit we can do much for your kingdom. We need to help one another and encourage each other. Be with us, Lord, and guide us in all that we do. Amen.

Prayer Of Confession
O God, we read in your Word that when you forgive our waywardness you will no longer remember our sins and evil deeds. We thank you for this undeserved and all-encompassing love and mercy. Encourage us by your Holy Spirit in the new life, the new opportunities, and the new determination to do your will that is ours. We pray in Jesus' name. Amen.

Hymns
"Lead On, O King Eternal"
"Where Charity And Love Prevail"

Third Sunday In November

Gospel Lesson: Mark 13:1-8
Theme: The Time Is Not Now

Call To Worship

Leader: Prepare to meet your Lord, for he will come at an hour when you least expect him.
People: We will do our best to be a people prepared for his coming.
Leader: Prepare your hearts and your minds. Study to show yourselves as those worthy of God's name.
People: We will strive to be children worthy of such a great God.

Collect

Lord, we know that no one can foretell when the end will come and your kingdom will come in all its wonder and glory. Meanwhile, we know that you come to each of us, and when we respond your kingdom has its beginning in our lives. Bless this time of worship that it may be a renewal of that faith. We pray in Jesus' name. Amen.

Prayer Of Confession

O God, we don't like to be kept in the dark. We want to be an insider who keeps up with all the latest information. Forgive our impatience, Lord, and teach us to live for today as though it were the last day. Help us to love and serve you with all our heart and mind and soul and strength. We pray in Jesus' name. Amen.

Hymns

"Behold A Broken World"
"Rejoice, The Lord Is King"

Fourth Sunday In November

First Lesson: Samuel 23:1-7
Theme: Hope For The Future

Call To Worship

Leader: Lift up your heads, O gates! and be lifted up, O ancient doors! that the King of glory may come in.
People: Who is the King of glory?
Leader: The Lord, strong and mighty, the Lord mighty in battle.
People: Lift up your heads, O gates! and be lifted up O ancient doors! that the King of glory may come in.
Leader: Who is this King of glory?
People: The Lord of hosts, he is the King of glory.

Collect

Sovereign God, Creator and Ruler of the universe, we do earnestly pray that your kingdom may come, and your will be done on earth as it is in heaven. Rule in our hearts through Jesus Christ so that we may glimpse the glory of your eternal realm, and as loyal disciples be used by you in the building of your kingdom. Amen.

Prayer Of Confession

Almighty God, you have called us to obey your commands, but we confess that there are times when we have been swayed by earthly rulers to support causes that we know are not in keeping with your ways. Grant us the courage to take our stand as citizens of your kingdom, and remind us of our pledge to uphold the cause of justice, peace, and goodwill among all peoples. Amen.

Hymns

"My Hope Is Built"
"Hope Of The World"

Fourth Sunday In November

Second Lesson: Revelation 1:4b-8
Theme: Christ, The Ruler Of The Earth

Call To Worship

Leader: "I am the Alpha and the Omega," says the Lord God, "who is, and who was, and who is to come, the Almighty."

People: Blessing and honor and glory and might be unto the Lamb, forever and ever!

Leader: Worthy is Christ who by his sacrificial death bought for God people from every tribe, language, nation, and race and made them a kingdom of priests to serve our God.

People: Holy, holy, holy is the Lord God Almighty, who was and is and is to come. Amen.

Collect

Eternal God, we give you thanks for your Son, Jesus Christ, who dwelt among us and opened to us the gates of your kingdom, a realm where all peoples, nations, and languages shall be included. Make us loyal followers of our living Lord, that we may follow his teachings, and live in his Spirit. We pray in his name. Amen.

Prayer Of Confession

Lord, where we have been hesitant to give you our full loyalty and devotion we seek your forgiveness. Relying on our own strength we know that we can never become the disciples that you would have us to be, and so we come seeking the power of your Holy Spirit to keep us ever faithful to you and your kingdom. Amen.

Hymns

"All Hail The Power Of Jesus' Name"
"Joy To The World"

Fourth Sunday In November

Gospel Lesson: John 18:33-37
Theme: Pilate Asked Jesus: "Are You A King, Then?"

Call To Worship
"All hail the power of Jesus' name. Let angels prostrate fall. Bring forth the royal diadem, and crown him Lord of all!"
Come, let us worship the King of kings, Lord of lords, Jesus Christ the everlasting Lord.

Collect
Almighty God, hasten the day when every knee shall bow and every tongue confess that Jesus Christ is Lord. Through this time of worship, O God, renew our enthusiasm and excitement, our commitment and hope for the coming of your kingdom. We pray in Jesus' name. Amen.

Prayer Of Confession
Gracious God, we rejoice in the message of your Son, Jesus Christ, that if we repent our sins will be forgiven. We thank you for the new life that is ours when we are freed from our sins. We pray that we may always seek your will and guidance as we strive to live as worthy citizens of your kingdom. Amen.

Hymns
"Rejoice, The Lord Is King"
"Ye Servants Of God"

Day Of Thanksgiving

First Lesson: Joel 2:21-27
Theme: The Lord Provides

Call To Worship

Leader: Let us thank the Lord for his steadfast love, for his wonderful works to all people.

People: The Lord is good to all, and his compassion is over all that he has made.

Leader: Blessed be the Lord, our God, who does wondrous things.

People: Blessed be his glorious name forever; may his glory fill the whole earth.

Collect

How good you have been to us, O God! You have blessed us with a rich and marvelous heritage in both our nation and our church. We are truly the recipients of blessings given to us by those who have been the pioneers of our faith and life here in America. Laws, freedom, truth, and faith in you have been given to us through the courage and commitment of our ancestors. We give thanks for this great heritage! Amen.

Prayer Of Confession

Heavenly Father, to count your many blessings to us would be like trying to count the stars. Forgive us for taking them for granted, and by the power of your Holy Spirit enable us to see that we have been blessed in order that we might be a blessing to others; through Jesus Christ our Lord. Amen.

Hymns

"Come, Ye Thankful People, Come"
"For The Beauty Of The Earth"

Day Of Thanksgiving

Second Lesson: 1 Timothy 2:1-7
Theme: Thanksgiving For All In Authority

Call To Worship
Leader: Let the nations be glad and sing for joy, for you judge the people with equity and guide all the nations upon the earth.
People: Let all the people praise you, O God; let all the people praise you.

Collect
Almighty God, we give you thanks for those who commit themselves to the task of government and leadership in the nations of the world, and particularly those in our own country. Give them a vision of truth and justice, that by their counsel all nations may work together in true brotherhood. Breathe into their hearts a new spirit of self-sacrifice that will enable them to work tirelessly for the welfare of all humankind. Amen.

Prayer Of Confession
Lord, we are always quick to criticize and slow to express our thanks. Not only do we seek your pardon for past failures, but we ask that your Spirit will motivate us to express our thanks through prayer and personal contact for those who faithfully serve you by serving in the halls of government. Amen.

Hymns
"Praise To The Lord, The Almighty"
"Now Thank We All Our God"

Day Of Thanksgiving

Gospel Lesson: Matthew 6:25-33
Theme: Do Not Worry

Call To Worship

Leader: Acknowledge that the Lord is God. He made us, and we belong to him.

People: We are his people, we are his flock.

Leader: Enter the Temple gates with thanksgiving; go into its courts with praise.

People: Give thanks to him and praise him.

Leader: The Lord is good, his love is eternal,

People: and his faithfulness lasts forever.

Collect

Our Father, we give you thanks that you have brought us through the circuit of another year, and you have kept your promise of seedtime and harvest. Despite drought, heavy rains, and freezing temperatures we have the assurance that there will be food enough for the coming year and seeds for planting in the spring. How fortunate we are to be able to live as we do. Thanks be to you, O God, thanks be to you! Amen.

Prayer Of Confession

Lord, while we enjoy the bounty of another harvest we know that there are some in our own land and many others throughout the world who go to bed hungry every night. Use us individually and as a church, we pray, to work at solutions to this problem. Let us not rest until the world's bountiful harvests are spread to include all those who hunger. In Christ's name we pray. Amen.

Hymns

"God Will Take Care Of You"
"We Gather Together"